Elizabeth Blackwell

with profiles of
Elizabeth Garrett Anderson
and Susan La Flesche Picotte

World Book, Inc.
a Scott Fetzer company
Chicago

BIOGRAPHICAL ⊕ CONNECTIONS

Writer: Lisa Klobuchar.

World Book, Inc.
233 N. Michigan Ave.
Chicago, IL 60601

For information about other World Book publications, visit our Web site at **www.worldbook.com** or call **1-800-WORLDBK (967-5325)**.
For information about sales to schools and libraries, call **1-800-975-3250 (United States)**, or **1-800-837-5365 (Canada)**.

Library of Congress Cataloging-in-Publication Data

Klobuchar, Lisa.
   Elizabeth Blackwell : with profiles of Elizabeth Garrett Anderson and Susan La Flesche Picotte / writer, Lisa Klobuchar.
      p. cm. -- (Biographical connections)
   Summary: "A biography of Elizabeth Blackwell, the first woman to obtain an M.D. degree in the United States, with profiles of two prominent individuals, who are associated through the influences they had on one another, the successes they achieved, or the goals they worked toward. Includes recommended readings and web sites"--Provided by publisher.
   Includes bibliographical references and index.
   ISBN-13: 978-0-7166-1826-3
   ISBN-10: 0-7166-1826-5
   1. Blackwell, Elizabeth, 1821-1910. 2. Women physicians--United States--Biography--Juvenile literature. 3. Anderson, Elizabeth Garrett, 1836-1917. 4. Picotte, Susan LaFlesche, 1865-1915. I. World Book, Inc. II. Title. III. Series.
   R692.K58 2007
   610.92'2--dc22
                          2006015739

Printed in the United States of America
1 2 3 4 5 10 09 08 07 06

Contents

Acknowledgments

The publisher gratefully acknowledges the following sources for the photographs in this volume.

Cover   Hobart and William Smith Colleges Archives
       Mary Evans Picture Library
       Nebraska State Historical Society

  7-11   Mary Evans Picture Library
    16   © Corbis/Hulton-Deutsch Collection
    18   Mary Evans Picture Library
    19   © Wellcome Library, London
    20   © Corbis/Bettmann
    22   © Wellcome Library, London
    25   Mary Evans Picture Library
    27   Granger Collection
    28   Illustrated London News Picture Library
 35-40   Library of Congress
    49   © Corbis/Bettmann
    58   Archives and Special Collections on Women in Medicine, Allegheny University of the Health Sciences
    62   © Wellcome Library, London
    66   © Corbis/Stapleton Collection
    71   © Corbis/Bettmann
 81-86   Library of Congress
89-104   Nebraska State Historical Society

Preface

Biographical Connections takes a contextual approach in presenting the lives of important people. In each volume, there is a biography of a central figure. This biography is preceded and followed by profiles of other individuals whose lifework connects in some way to that of the central figure. The three subjects are associated through the influences they had on one another, the successes they achieved, or the goals they worked toward. The series includes men and women from around the world and throughout history in a variety of fields.

Today, women doctors work in every field of medicine throughout the world. But between 1900 and the 1960's, only about 5 percent of doctors in the United States were women. As recently as 1983, the profession was still overwhelmingly dominated by men. At that time only 16 percent of physicians in the United States were women. Even though this number has risen steadily since the 1980's, by 2003, only 30 percent of physicians in the United States were women. Today, the chief challenge of female doctors is not gaining acceptance in the profession. Instead, it is a challenge similar to that facing women in other professions—how to balance a demanding career with a private life that may include raising children and running a home.

But 150 years ago, women wishing to enter the medical profession in the United States and Great Britain confronted formidable barriers. Women were believed to be physically and intellectually inferior to men. They were seen as incapable of understanding complex scientific or philosophical concepts and prone to emotional excesses when cool rationality was needed. Moreover, the female body and and its functions were seen as making them unfit for any activities that required strength or stamina. Also, women were believed to have almost sacred roles as mothers, wives, homemakers, and caretakers from which they should not be distracted. These attitudes combined to create an atmosphere in which any woman who tried to pursue a career outside the home was considered a serious threat to the very fabric of society. Not only men, but many women also, denounced the dangerous and unnatural designs of women who pursued a career.

It was in this atmosphere that the three women profiled in this volume made their forays into the medical profession. In 1849, Elizabeth Blackwell became the first woman to earn the M.D. degree in the United States. In 1870, Elizabeth Garrett Anderson became the first British woman to earn the degree. Through determination, strength of will and character, and unwavering belief in themselves and the importance of their goals, they overcame the tremendous obstacles that stood in the way of all women who dared step out of the ideal of womanhood during the 1800's.

The story of Susan La Flesche Picotte, the first Native American woman doctor, is a little different. By the time she entered medical school, in 1886, several women's medical schools operated in the United States and Great Britain. Picotte battled the United States government's policies, which deprived Native Americans of their land and traditional livelihoods. As a physician on the Omaha reservation in Nebraska, she contended not only with lack of funding and inadequate supplies; she also tried to save her people from the ravages of alcoholism, which she saw as a direct result of U.S. Native American policies. As a representative and advocate for the Omaha, she also worked to prevent white land purchasers from defrauding the Omaha and to change U.S. government policies and bureaucratic red tape that she believed harmed her people.

These three women had very different backgrounds. Blackwell, though born into comfortable upper-middle class circumstances, knew economic hardship throughout most of her life. Anderson grew up in a well-to-do family, and lived most of her life in prosperity. As a Native American, Susan La Flesche Picotte was a member of a marginalized group—as such, she had neither money nor family connections to help her along. For all their differences, however, Blackwell, Anderson, and Picotte had one significant advantage in common: each of them was given direction, instruction, support, and encouragement by fathers who believed that their daughters should have the same education and freedom as their sons. Within the hearts and minds of all three of these women was the confidence—largely bestowed upon them by their fathers—that they could succeed in any area of life they chose. And all three did succeed, magnificently. ■

Elizabeth Garrett Anderson (1836–1917)

"In great haste I write you a few lines touching the medical event of the day—to wit the reception of Miss Garrett as an M.D. of the Paris Faculty, which has just this instant taken place and in which I had the pleasure of assisting. . . . The hall was literally crowded with students, and, on Miss Garrett's crossing the courtyard to leave the school, I observed with pleasure that almost all the students gallantly bowed to their lady confrère. All the judges, on complimenting Miss Garrett, more or less expressed liberal opinions on the subject of lady doctors, and one Professor M. Broca was especially energetic and enthusiastic. Altogether there was an air of fête about the Faculty."[1]

So emoted the Paris correspondent for the British medical journal *The Lancet*, describing the glorious turning point in the career of Elizabeth Garrett Anderson, England's first female medical doctor. But the road leading up to this triumph was long and hard, and the road ahead would bring still more achievements.

EARLY LIFE

Elizabeth Garrett was born in London, on June 9, 1836, the second child of Newson Garrett and his wife, Louisa. Elizabeth's older sister, Louisa, had been born 16 months earlier. The family lived in Whitechapel, a poor gritty neighborhood, where Newson Garrett ran a pawnshop, offering small loans in exchange for personal property. Garrett was an ambitious young man and had no intention of remaining a pawnbroker all his life. In 1840, he moved with his family to the seaside town of

Aldeburgh in Suffolk. The family now included two boys, Newson and Edmund. By the 1850's the family would grow to include a total of 10 children.

Garrett chose as his business the malting of grain. Malted grain was an ingredient in beer brewing. He was very competitive with his older brother, who was enjoying enormous success in manufacturing agricultural tools and machinery, and he worked energetically to build his own business empire. Garrett's empire grew quickly. Within a few years, he owned a fleet of ships, which transported his malted grain, as well as coal, to London and other English cities.

So from her earliest days, Elizabeth was exposed to her father's drive, ingenuity, boldness, and success at everything he turned his hand to. Elizabeth also benefited from her father's liberal ideas with regard to childrearing. It was the norm during that time among the middle- and upper-middle class in England that children, especially girls, needed to be sheltered from life in the bigger world. But Garrett allowed all his children to explore the seashore, the countryside, the docks, and to freely mingle with the townspeople, no matter if their station were "inferior" to the family's own.

Elizabeth's and Louisa's early education came from their mother, who taught them the basic three-R's at home. When Elizabeth was 10, the family hired a governess by the name of Miss Edgeworth to teach the older girls. Miss Edgeworth's timid, fawning agreeableness and her lack of intellectual spark bored and infuriated the bright and lively Elizabeth. Elizabeth coped with the situation by devising ways to embarrass and outsmart her governess. This unfortunate situation continued for three years, until Garrett decided that his daughters needed a better education. So they were sent off to a boarding school for young women in Blackheath, a section of London. They received

Newson Garrett supported his daughter's decision to become a medical doctor. Elizabeth Garrett was influenced early on by her father's drive, ingenuity, boldness, and determination to succeed.

probably the best sort of education that could be expected for young girls at the time, for it was the common attitude that education was wasted on girls, who were expected to become dutiful wives and mothers when they grew up, and to have no careers and take no part in public life.

Another benefit of their time at boarding school was the lifelong friendships they made there. Louisa became friends with two sisters of the Smith family, whose brother she would eventually marry, and Elizabeth became pals with Jane Crowe, who would later become secretary of the Society for Promoting the Employment of Women. After about two years, the Garrett sisters finished their boarding school education. Though Elizabeth's entire future life would depend on her furthering her education, this was the only time she would be enrolled officially in school. Back home, she took the initiative to independently continue her education. She studied Latin and math with her brother Newson's tutor, and read constantly.

CAREER INSPIRATION

In 1854, Louisa and Elizabeth paid a visit to their school friends Jane and Annie Crowe, whom they had met at boarding school. While there, they met another young woman, named Emily Davies. Emily was frustrated with the lack of opportunities for young women. Kindred spirits, the young women banded together to come up with ways that they could create opportunities for themselves. For Elizabeth it was the beginning of a search for a purpose in life. Later she would say about this period of her life: "I was a young woman living at home with nothing to do in what authors call 'comfortable circumstances.' But I was wicked enough not to be comfortable. I was full of energy and vigour and of the discontent which goes with unemployed activities."[2]

Another key event around this time was the first publication of a magazine called the *Englishwoman's Journal*, which advocated a larger role for women in employment and public life. The magazine regularly featured profiles on prominent women. It was possible that Elizabeth first read in the journal about the British-born American female physician, Elizabeth Blackwell, who in 1849, had become the first woman medical doctor in the United States. In 1859, she heard that Dr. Blackwell would be visiting England.

In March 1859, Elizabeth went to hear Dr. Blackwell give the first of a scheduled three lectures on "Medicine as a Profession for Ladies." Blackwell echoed many of Elizabeth's most cherished longings when she spoke of meaningful employment giving women "the feeling of belonging to the world in fact instead of a crippled and isolated life."[3] After the lecture, Elizabeth met the eminent doctor at a party at Barbara Bodichon's home. Much to Elizabeth's surprise, Dr. Blackwell talked to her as though Elizabeth had committed to pursuing a career in medicine, when in fact, the idea had never crossed her mind. Moreover, little did Elizabeth know it at the time, but Dr. Blackwell would become and remain one of her supporters and friends to the end of the older doctor's life.

During the next several weeks, Elizabeth attended two more of Dr. Blackwell's lectures. Emily Davies and Elizabeth enthusiastically discussed the possibility of Elizabeth studying medicine. Emily Davies was especially keen on the idea and encouraged her friend with persuasive arguments of the need for women doctors to care for women and children. By the time Elizabeth returned home to Aldeburgh, she had made up her mind to become a doctor.

AN UPHILL CLIMB

First, with Emily's help, Elizabeth analyzed her position. Through an article by Elizabeth Blackwell in the *Englishwoman's Journal*, they learned of all the years of rigorous education and hard-to-obtain—for women—practical experience required for becoming a doctor, as well as the expense involved. For the time being, Elizabeth thought it best not to reveal her plans to her father, whose support she knew would be indispensable.

Instead, she discreetly began her education. She enlisted the help of the Aldeburgh schoolmaster in her study of Latin and Greek. She wrote English compositions for Emily Davies to critique. By June of 1860, Elizabeth decided the time had come to inform her father of her plans.

His reaction was vocal and unequivocal. In a letter to Emily, Elizabeth describes his reaction: "He said the whole idea was so *disgusting*, that he could not entertain it for a moment!"[4] Elizabeth offered arguments to persuade him. If it were not disgusting for women to be nurses, why should it be different for them to become doctors? She told him how important it was to her to find a meaningful career. His position softened somewhat. He told her he would give it more thought.

Elizabeth's plans became a topic of family discussions for the next couple of weeks, with divided opinions. Her mother was so upset by the idea she cried herself sick. But ultimately it was Mr. Garrett's blessing and support Elizabeth needed, and she soon got it. He agreed to travel with her to London to consult with medical practitioners.

Getting a medical education would not be a problem, they learned, as long as Mr. Garrett were willing to spend his money on tutors and lectures. But no medical school would allow her to get clinical practice. And to practice medicine legally, she would need to take examinations for a license. Not a single medical board—they were told again and again—would allow a woman to take such exams.

A force working in Elizabeth's favor, it turns out, was her father's proud, contrary spirit. The thought that anyone dared suggest that he or one of his own were not allowed to do something they were fully capable of doing brought out the fighting spirit in him. He decided to fully support Elizabeth in her ambitions: "I have resolved in my own mind after deep and painful consideration not to oppose your wishes and views and as far as expense is involved I will do all I can, in justice to my other children, to assist you in your study."[5]

In the meantime, Elizabeth had found some new allies. She was introduced to William Hawes, who sat on the board of Middlesex Hospital, an old and well-respected institution in London, which had a medical school. He suggested that Elizabeth should work for a time as a surgical nurse in order to familiarize herself with medical practice. She agreed. In August 1860, she started work at Middlesex Hospital in London, embarking on her first step in her medical education. In a sense, she would be masquerading as a nurse while learning the routines of surgical work, which at that time mostly involved amputations and was a filthy and laborious job.

She spent her busy days in the surgical ward, preparing bandages and medicines to be applied to wounds. She accompanied one of the experienced nurses on the rounds, changing bandages and doling out medicines, and observed the doctors as they treated patients. She spent her spare time reading.

A few of the physicians, impressed by her quick mind and her cool demeanor in the face of the gore of the operating room, treated her with respect and taught her as they would any other student. But before long she began to be made aware of just how lacking she was in educational background for medical study. As a young woman, her early education did not include the science basics—chemistry, physics, anatomy, and physiology. She arranged to receive tutoring in Latin, and the study of medicines with the hospital pharmacist, Joshua Plaskitt. The young *house* (resident) physician, Dr. Willis, also agreed to tutor her. She also convinced the nursing staff to allow her to perform night duty unsupervised. After three months at Middlesex, the nurses and medical staff, and even—for the time being—the young medical students, had accepted her as an unofficial medical student.

By March 1861, Elizabeth had obtained permission to attend lectures in chemistry and to participate in dissections. She was a bright student, the instructors were impressed and helpful, and her confidence grew.

Elizabeth had friends and allies on the hospital staff and her knowledge and skill were growing by leaps and bounds. But the reality of life during the 1800's was that a woman medical student was perhaps something to be tolerated in a spirit of generosity tinged with amusement, but was not to be accepted on equal terms with males. She passed all her examinations with honors, and when she was given the news she was asked to keep it a secret from the other students.

In early June, Elizabeth and the medical students were making the rounds with a visiting physician. At the bed of one patient, the physician asked the students a question about the case. The male students stood by in silence. None of them knew the answer. But Elizabeth did, and she gave it with her usual matter-of-fact coolness.

"Young females . . . in the operating theatre is an outrage on our natural instincts and feelings and calculated to destroy those sentiments of respect and admiration with which the opposite sex is regarded by all right minded men."

Memo from male medical students to medical school committee, Middlesex Hospital, London, 1861

Elizabeth did not know it, but this exceeded the tolerance of the medical students. They would not permit themselves to be shown up by a woman. A group of students met and quickly drew up a memo outlining their case. Within days, the medical school committee met to consider the students' demands. The students did not say that the reason for their vote was competitiveness and professional jealousy. Instead they made their argument by citing the impropriety of mixing men and women in the study of medicine. Their formal letter outlining their reasons read in part: "Young females . . . in the operating theatre is an outrage on our natural instincts and feelings and calculated to destroy those sentiments of respect and admiration with which the opposite sex is regarded by all right minded men."[6] The committee's vote in favor of the students was not unanimous; Elizabeth had some genuine allies. But the majority ruled. No amount of appealing could change the male students' determination to be rid of her. After the remaining weeks of the term ended, so did her stay at Middlesex.

A CAMPAIGN FOR EQUAL OPPORTUNITY

Throughout the summer, Elizabeth applied to and was rejected by a number of medical schools in London. She wrote to several organizations that administered examinations and issued licenses to practice medicine. She wanted to know if she would be permitted to take their license exams. All but one of these organizations refused. But in August, she received good news. The Society of Apothecaries, a legal examining board in England, agreed to let her take its licensing exam once she fulfilled its requirements. Licensed apothecaries were legally allowed to practice medicine. It was the least prestigious of all medical licenses, but it was the only one open to Elizabeth.

She had many classes to complete before she could even qualify to take the examination. Her goal was to enter a university, so she spent the fall studying Latin and Greek. She also attended lectures on botany, physics, natural history, and physiology, which were some of the course requirements for the apothecary's exam. In the spring of 1862, she asked for permission to be allowed to enroll in the University of London. There was little disagreement about whether she was qualified. She clearly was. But the charter of the school prohibited women, and therefore she could not be admitted. There was some support, however, for changing the university's charter to remove this prohibition.

So Elizabeth began her campaign. She enlisted help from Emily Davies and her influential acquaintances, and they wrote to the members of the university senate and to newspapers and journals. They distributed 1,500 copies of a pamphlet outlining the reasons why women should be admitted to the university. But once again, the tide of public opinion was against her. The senate refused to change the charter by only one vote.

Elizabeth next turned her attention to the universities in the rest of England and in Scotland, but the result was similar. It appeared that she could not receive a formal higher education of any kind in Great Britain. She went to Scotland in the fall, hoping to enroll in St. Andrews. When this failed, she studied privately with George Day, an eminent professor of anatomy and physiology, for the winter term. Then she made private arrangements to attend lectures at the University of Edinburgh and studied with Alexander Keiller, a professor and physician in obstetrics and gynecology. Under Keiller, she received valuable clinical experience at the Edinburgh Maternity Hospital, where she assisted at 12 births and observed close to 100 others.

By autumn 1863, she was back in London, learning the intricacies of the human body in the dissection room. She studied under the direction of a brilliant 23-year-old surgeon named L. S. Little, the only anatomist in London who would accept her as a student. To gain the hands-on clinical experience she needed, she once again had to resort to applying as a nursing student. In early 1864, she began her training at the London Hospital, a 400-bed facility located in an impoverished neighborhood very close to her birthplace. There she focused on obstetrics and vaccination, and her chief instructor, a young doctor named Nathaniel Heckford, allowed her to independently diagnose cases and suggest treatments. By the time she finished her six-month term, she had independently attended 55 births.

A few months later, Elizabeth resumed her study of anatomy with Little, and returned to Middlesex Hospital for further clinical training. Again, the hospital refused to admit her officially but allowed her to attend rounds with whichever individual doctors permitted it. She left in March 1865, her clinical requirements for the Society of Apothecaries license completed. By the fall, she finished her course requirements.

On Sept. 28, 1865, she showed up at Apothecaries' Hall for the licensing examination. Of all the persons who took the test, Elizabeth's score was the highest. After more than five years of hard work, clambering over obstacle upon obstacle, suffering setbacks that only her extraordinary confidence, patience, and persistence enabled her to overcome, she was now licensed to practice medicine in the United Kingdom.

Elizabeth's father would not abandon his daughter now. As he had throughout her difficult years of study, he provided her with an allowance to set up a household and small office. She saw patients under the title L.S.A., or Licentiate of the Society of Apothecaries. Her practice grew slowly but steadily.

In 1866, Elizabeth opened St. Mary's Dispensary for Women and Children. Within a few months of its opening, the clinic was serving between 60 to 90 women a day. She treated poor women, their bodies worn out by years of hard living and childbirth, and prostitutes whose lives were unimaginably tragic. All these women must have found immense comfort and relief having a female physician to whom they could pour out their hearts.

In September, she became the second woman, after Elizabeth Blackwell, to have her name—Elizabeth Garrett, L.S.A.—entered on the British Medical Register.

Elizabeth Garrett's career was progressing and her dispensary was busy. She was invited to give lectures and submit articles to magazines. Her influence grew. But in 1867 tragedy struck very close to home. Her beloved sister Louisa became ill with appendicitis.

In March 1869, Garrett took her first examination for the medical degree at the Faculty of Medicine in Paris. She sat in a large hall at a long table across from the medical examiners for the oral exam. Medical students, faculty, and supporters filled the hall and burst into applause when Garrett responded correctly to each question.

Although today appendicitis is routinely treated by surgically removing the infected organ, at that time there was no treatment. Within a short time of falling ill, Louisa died. "Our darling is gone, and we can never get a word or a look from her again!"[7] Elizabeth said.

Her grief was deep and heartfelt. Louisa had been her supporter, companion, and kindred spirit her entire life. Her kindness and gentleness balanced Elizabeth's singleminded and sometimes self-centered drive. Elizabeth had to go on as best she could without her touchstone.

But she still had her work, and now a new opportunity had opened up for her. In 1868, it had been announced that France would grant women M.D. degrees. Garrett, who was fluent in French, saw her opportunity. She did not feel she needed, nor did she want, further medical education. She simply wanted to take the examinations in Paris to earn the degree.

She arrived in Paris for her first exam in March 1869. The examinations were oral. She sat in a large hall at a long table across from three examiners. The hall was filled with an audience made up of curious—and supportive—medical students and faculty. When she answered her questions quickly and correctly, the room burst into applause. She passed the first exam with flying colors.

She returned to Paris in June for the second part of the exam, in which she had to perform two surgeries while under the observation of the examiners and spectators and then take another oral examination. She passed this one with high marks also. During additional trips she passed her third, fourth, and fifth exams and handed her thesis, on migraine, to the medical faculty.

Garrett's next professional milestone would also lead to a major personal milestone. Her old tutor in obstetrics at the London Hospital, Nathaniel Heckford, had founded a children's hospital in 1867. In March 1870, he invited Elizabeth to become the hospital's visiting medical officer. The hospital board, which was made up of both physicians and laymen, was divided in their opinion of the appointment. One member of the board, James G. Skelton Anderson, was one of the skeptics, feeling that the job was too demanding for a woman. But at her interview, he had a change of

James G. Skelton Anderson, a board member of a children's hospital in London, was skeptical when Elizabeth Garrett was invited to become the hospital's visiting medical officer in March 1870. But after her interview, not only did he vote for her appointment, in less than a year they were married.

mind. Not only did he vote for her appointment, but less than a year later he would become her husband. Their courtship started out as a friendship based on professional duties and ambitions.

But in the meantime, there was the final step in her Paris M.D. to take care of. In June, she stood before the medical faculty of Sorbonne College (now the University of Paris). She read her thesis aloud and took the last of her oral examinations. When she passed, she made history as the first woman to earn a medical degree from the Sorbonne. The British medical press, still fervently opposed to the idea of female doctors, at least praised her "perseverance and pluck."[8]

Garrett returned to England with the right, finally, to use the title "Doctor," although she chose never to use the title. In her duties at the children's hospital, she found more and more that Anderson was a kindred spirit and an ally. They both worked to keep the hospital on firm ground, financially, hygienically, and organizationally. Together they fought wars on fleas, revamped the way medications were bought and stored, and successfully ousted an incompetent physician whom Heckford had appointed.

Their friendship, mutual admiration, and respect grew, but it was probably cemented over the course of events during the fall of 1870. That year a new British law had provided for public elementary schools administered by school boards. A group of husbands and fathers of her dispensary patients petitioned her to run for the board in their district. Though hesitant to take a position that would require her to be in the public eye, she agreed to run on the condition that her good friend and colleague Anderson be her campaign chairman. Together they made a good team. On the voting day, November 30, in a field of seven candidates, she received about 43 percent of the votes, outdistancing the second-place candidate by more than 34,000 votes.

On December 23, Anderson proposed and the two were married on Feb. 9, 1871. They would have three children: Louisa, born in

1873; Margaret, born in 1874, and who died of meningitis at the age of 15 months; and Alan, born in 1877.

THE NEW HOSPITAL FOR WOMEN

By 1872, it was time to expand the dispensary. Anderson's reputation had grown and now women from all over London wanted to be treated by a female doctor. Sometimes even very ill women would travel long distances to come to the clinic. She saw the need for a hospital that could handle *inpatients* (patients who cannot remain at home). She opened her new hospital in February 1872 in the same building as the dispensary. It was named the New Hospital for Women, it had 10 beds, and it was the first hospital for women staffed entirely by women. In 1874, the New Hospital for Women moved into bigger quarters and expanded to 26 beds.

Elizabeth routinely performed surgery, and was one of the first physicians to practice newly discovered antiseptic techniques. When Elizabeth began her medical training at Middlesex Hospital 12 years before, the relationship between infection and germs was not understood. Doctors performed dissections on cadavers with students.

Anderson opened the New Hospital for Women in London in February 1872. It had 10 beds and was the first hospital for women staffed entirely by women. In 1874, the hospital moved into bigger quarters and expanded to 26 beds. It is now named the Elizabeth Garrett Anderson Hospital. The hospital is shown in a photo taken around 1916.

Then later, wearing the very same coats, they operated on living patients. Moreover, the coats were never washed. The stiffened, blood-stained coats were in a sense a mark of their experience and prowess as surgeons. Doctors kept needles and thread for closing surgical wounds at the ready stuck in the lapels of their coats. No one knew that the threads, trailing on the ground, the scalpels and other instruments that were used and reused on patient after patient without washing, and the physicians' hands and clothing were the source of the deadly infections that took the lives of many patients. They did not know that simple sanitary methods could make the difference between life and death for many patients.

But in 1865, Sir Joseph Lister, a British physician, had used French chemist Louis Pasteur's discovery that germs caused disease to figure out that the formation of pus was also due to germs. As a result of unsanitary practices, the most trivial operation was likely to be followed by infection, and death occurred in up to 50 percent of all surgical cases. Lister discovered that carbolic acid sprays could be used to kill germs and that antiseptics could kill germs on surgeons' hands, instruments, dressings, and on patients.

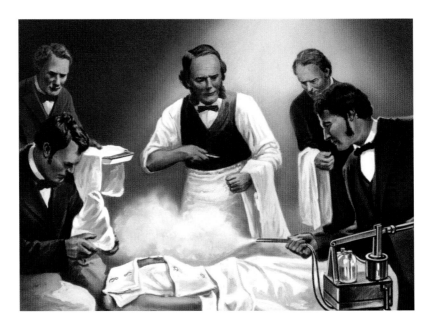

British physician Joseph Lister, center, in apron, *founded antiseptic surgery in 1865. He is shown directing the use of carbolic acid spray to kill germs in the air during surgery. Elizabeth Garrett Anderson was one of the first physicians to adopt Lister's antiseptic practices in all her surgeries, leading to a decrease in infection.*

Anderson was one of the first physicians to adopt these practices in all her surgeries, leading to a decrease in infection. She used them when she most likely became the first female surgeon in Europe to surgically remove an ovary. Among the various gynecological disorders treated surgically were *uterine fibroids* (noncancerous growths on the uterine wall), *uterine prolapse* (slipping of the uterus from its normal position), cancer, and ovarian tumors. These surgeries tested her confidence. Years later she observed that a trained surgeon could make the work seem easy, but only the experience of actually performing surgery revealed how much nerve it required. She wrote: "I believe it is impossible for any but those who have gone through it to realize what a tremendous tax upon one's nerve is to attempt a great operation, especially of the kind where exact previous knowledge of the difficulties cannot possibly be had."[9]

The birth of Elizabeth and James's first child, Louisa, in 1873, added to Elizabeth's many responsibilities, and she decided to reduce her activities. She decided not to run for reelection to the school board, and she resigned from the children's hospital.

A great boon to her career occurred a few months later when she was elected to the British Medical Association. The association's charter at that time did not specifically exclude women. Because Anderson met all qualifications, she was elected. However, she would remain the only women on the register for years to come because in 1878, despite her efforts to the contrary, the membership voted to exclude women. But they allowed Anderson to remain on the register. Other women doctors would have to wait until 1892 before the British Medical Association would admit them.

THE LONDON SCHOOL OF MEDICINE FOR WOMEN

In 1874, Sophia Jex-Blake, an old acquaintance of Anderson's, began an effort to open a women's medical school in London. The two women had had an uneasy relationship for over a decade. Though they worked for the same causes—equal opportunities for women in education and medicine—Jex-Blake had a fiery, impetuous personality and a tendency to be defensive and overly emotional in the face of opposition. She often failed in her causes because of poor timing, intemperate remarks in public, and the alienation of would-be supporters. Anderson could not give her support to Sophia. She felt that providing a separate medical education for women in Great Britain would open up graduates to accusations of inferiority. She believed that British women who wanted a medical degree should get it abroad and then return to England to practice. In this way, women would demonstrate that they were fully qualified to be doctors, and existing all-male medical schools would eventually open their doors to women.

But Jex-Blake persisted in her efforts to found a women's medical college, and it soon became clear that this time she would succeed. Anderson felt she had no choice but to support it. She joined the school's permanent council and was one of its lecturers when the London School of Medicine for Women opened its doors in October 1874.

Anderson was lecturer and permanent council member of the London School of Medicine for Women, founded by Sophia Jex-Blake, when the school opened in October 1874. She served as dean of the school for 20 years. This photo shows women students at work in the school's physiology laboratory in 1899.

For the next several years Anderson maintained her private practice, ran her hospital, and taught at the women's medical college. In 1883, A. T. Norton, the male physician who had served as dean since the school's founding, resigned, and Anderson was appointed to replace him. Over the next several years enrollment grew, and during the mid-1880's Anderson oversaw the purchase of a building next door to expand the facilities.

The New Hospital for Women continued to grow, too, and it was faced with the loss of its home in 1887, when the owner of the buildings declined to renew the lease. By the next year, a site was found near the London School of Medicine for Women, where a new hospital would be built. Construction began under the constant, watchful eye of Elizabeth Garrett Anderson. In 1890, a brand-new New Hospital for Women opened, now with 42 beds.

In 1892, Anderson decided it was time to turn her surgical duties over to the younger doctors who would lead the hospital into the future. She resigned from the visiting staff and asked that Mary Scharlieb, a talented doctor who had become her student in 1878, and who had filled in for her capably over the years, be appointed to succeed her.

Though tinged with sorrow, the 1890's were years of continued success for Elizabeth and James. In May 1893, Elizabeth's father, Newson Garrett, died. In his will, he left her the family home and the grounds surrounding it. In 1896, Elizabeth was elected president of the East Anglican Branch of the British Medical Association.

The same year, enrollment at the London School of Medicine for Women had swelled to 159, and the student body had outgrown its present campus. Under Anderson's leadership, a bigger school was built at the same location. Construction began in 1897. Anderson resigned as lecturer to devote the majority of her time to overseeing the project. She also started another expansion of the New Hospital for Women at the same time. The new college officially opened on July 11, 1898. Elizabeth Blackwell was among the 250 female physicians who attended the opening ceremony. A few years later, the school would become a college within the University of London.

SENIOR CITIZEN SUFFRAGETTE

In 1903, Anderson retired as dean of the London School of Medicine for Women, after serving in that post for 20 years. She and James moved permanently back to Aldeburgh, and Elizabeth remained active on the councils of the New Hospital for Women and the London School of Medicine for Women. She also spent the next several years traveling and writing. She published papers and lectures detailing the history of women in medicine, supporting smallpox vaccination, examining the ethical problem of *vivisection* (medical experimentation on animals), and chronicling advances in medicine during the 1800's.

In 1907, James died while serving as mayor of Aldeburgh. Elizabeth was asked to run for the office. She won the election in 1908, adding first woman mayor in England to her list of illustrious firsts. Over the years her seaside hometown had developed into a popular vacation spot, and she worked hard to ensure that the area's infrastructure—its streets, water system, pier, street lighting, and green spaces—be improved to encourage this important source of income. She served as mayor until 1910.

Ever since she was a young woman, Anderson had been a firm supporter of women's *suffrage*—the right to vote. Her younger sister Millicent had been a leader in this movement since her early 20's. Though Elizabeth's medical and educational work did not leave her time for much active work on the cause, she did what she could. Now a widow, with many years of success and much respect and influence, she became more directly active in the cause. She befriended younger suffrage activists and on Oct. 18, 1908, at the age of 72, she joined a group of women in a march on Parliament. This was no ordinary peaceful gathering of women politely asking for their right to vote. On the contrary, these women were prepared to enter Parliament by force and be hauled off to jail if need be. Police scuffled with the impassioned women. Anderson, however, under advance warning to police, was not bothered. She took part in such demonstrations for the next three years. Women would not receive full voting rights in England until 1928.

Elizabeth Garrett Anderson, shown walking second in the procession, *became England's first woman mayor when she was elected mayor of Aldeburgh in 1908.*

After 1912, Anderson's health and her mental sharpness began to grow dull. She diagnosed herself with hardening of the arteries, which, she quipped, means "softening of the brain."[10] She began to grow more and more forgetful, alternating, in the way of many old people, good days with not-so-good days. Eventually, she became an invalid in a wheelchair. On Dec. 17, 1917, at the age of 81, she died.

Thanks to the example and influence of pioneering women like Elizabeth Garrett Anderson and her contemporaries, more and more women during the late 1800's and early 1900's defeated traditional restrictions on their activities and took their place in public and professional life. ■

Chronology of Blackwell's life

1821	born on February 3 in Counterslip, Gloucestershire, England
1847	begins medical studies at Geneva College in Geneva, New York
1848	admitted to the Philadelphia hospital of the Blockley Almshouse
1849	publishes thesis stressing importance of sanitation and personal hygiene in fighting disease; becomes first woman in U.S. to receive M.D. degree; becomes naturalized American citizen; becomes student midwife at La Maternité in Paris; loses left eye due to infection contracted from patient
1850	gains first clinical practice at St. Bartholomew's Hospital in London
1852	*The Laws of Life with Special Reference to the Physical Education of Girls* published
1853	opens free dispensary for poor patients near Tomkins Square in New York City
1857	opens New York Infirmary for Women and Children
1858	becomes first woman to have her name entered in the British Medical Registry
1859	gives lecture in London where she meets Elizabeth Garrett and inspires her to become England's first woman medical doctor
1861	becomes chair of registration committee of the Woman's Central Association of Relief
1868	establishes Woman's Medical College of the New York Infirmary
1871	adopts 7-year-old orphan Katharine Barry
1874	becomes council member of London School of Medicine for Women, founded by Sophia Jex-Blake
1875	appointed chair of gynecology at London School of Medicine for Women
1879	*Counsel to Parents on the Moral Education of Their Children* published
1895	autobiography *Pioneer Work in Opening the Medical Profession to Women* published
1910	dies May 31 in Hastings, Sussex, England

Elizabeth Blackwell (1821–1910)

In 1902, at the age of 81, while returning home to Hastings, England, from a vacation in Scotland, Elizabeth Blackwell and her adopted daughter, Kitty, visited Blackwell's birthplace and childhood home, Bristol, England. It had been 70 years since she had left. The visit was disappointing to the old woman, as she recorded in her journal: "Walked through Nelson St.—Bridwell Bridge, the Barton up Park St. to Kingsdown Parade, intending to go to Mother Pugsley's Fields, but found them all swept away and covered with houses—indeed the whole town is so completely changed, even Father's Sugar House, that the town was to me no longer recognisable, and seemed to have lost all interest for me. I found the searching and walking made the brain weary."[1]

The changes Blackwell observed in the town of her childhood were symbolic of the changes she experienced in her own life, as she overcame monumental social, educational, and professional barriers to become the first woman in medicine. The work of Elizabeth Blackwell and her example would effect far-reaching changes in medicine, education, and society throughout the world.

Elizabeth Blackwell was born near Bristol, England, in 1821. When she returned to visit 70 years later, in 1902, she found it as changed as the times in which she had grown up there. Bristol is shown in a 1902 engraving.

Chapter 1: From the Old World to the New

Elizabeth Blackwell was born on Feb. 3, 1821, the third of nine surviving children born to Samuel Blackwell, a sugar refiner, and his wife, Hannah, in Counterslip, near Bristol, Gloucestershire, England. She joined two older sisters, Anna and Marian. Elizabeth was a tiny baby, and her parents, after having lost an infant son the year before, were in fear for her life. Though the little girl lived, she would remain tiny even into adulthood, growing only to five feet one inch tall. Her two older sisters were dark-haired and outgoing, like their mother. Elizabeth was pale, with fine blond hair and gray eyes, like her father.

She often felt like the odd one out. Anna and Marian were close in age. Elizabeth's position in the birth order was between two boys who had both died as babies. The two younger surviving brothers closest in age to Elizabeth, Samuel and Henry, formed a duo, as did her younger sisters, Emily and Ellen, and the two youngest of the family, Howard and George. Among the nine, only Elizabeth had no sibling close to her age to pair with. Instead, she often joined with Anna and Marian, and the oldest daughters formed a group of three.

"LITTLE SHY"

But even if she had had social moorings within the family, young Elizabeth's personality set her apart from the others. Like her father, she was stubborn, high-principled, independent, driven, and perhaps most striking, reserved. It was her father who gave her the nickname "Little Shy." Father and daughter were devoted to each other. In her autobiography, published in 1895, she wrote that her "dear father, with his warm affection, his sense of fun, and his talent for rhyming, represented a beneficent Providence to me from my earliest recollection."[1]

The household also included her father's unmarried sisters: her aunts Ann, Lucy, Mary, and Barbara. The stern Barbara, self-appointed law enforcer, judge, and jury in the family, kept an accounting of all sins and transgressions in a small ledger, her infamous "Black Book." Elizabeth's tendency to do things her own way landed her name in the Black Book more often than her siblings and made her subject to her Aunt Barbara's punishments, often banishment to the attic, sometimes during eagerly anticipated social gatherings. These punishments contributed to her sense that she was somehow especially stained with sin.

A condition that disturbed Elizabeth's conscience was slavery. Her father's livelihood was sugar refining, and the raw material, sugar cane, was grown and harvested in the West Indies by slaves. Yet, he was fiercely opposed to slavery. Samuel Blackwell struggled constantly with the moral inconsistency between his beliefs and his business activities. The Blackwell children shared his abhorrence of slavery. Though their family livelihood depended on it, they gave up eating sugar because it was a slave product. The family was also religious, and Elizabeth was introduced from her earliest childhood to the concept of repentance for sin. In order to wipe her sins clean, she modeled her atonement on the methods used by the saints, specifically mortification of the flesh, or deliberate, self-imposed physical suffering. In Elizabeth's case it meant leaving her comfortable bed to sleep on the hard floor and denying herself food.

But her determination and denial of weakness, in body or will, set her apart further. When she got sick, she refused to give in. Instead of going to bed to recuperate, or going to the doctor, she convinced herself that she could cure herself by force of will alone. Later, while attending school in New York City, when she was a teen-ager, she attempted to get rid of a fever by walking it off.

AN OUTSIDER

Elizabeth must have felt like an outsider in other important ways as well, ways that were probably shared by all members of the family. First of all, Samuel and Hannah belonged to a religious group known as Dissenters. The national church of England is the Church of England. Dissenters were Protestants who belonged to other churches. Because of their religious affiliation,

Dissenters were not allowed to hold high government offices or work as physicians, attorneys, or professors. They were also barred from British universities. Most significant for the Blackwell children, Dissenters could not attend most regular elementary and high schools. As a result, they were isolated from other children and had to be educated at home by governesses and tutors.

This situation probably benefited the Blackwell children, especially Elizabeth and her sisters, in the long run. Samuel Blackwell was a reform-minded, progressive thinker. During the Victorian Age—named for the reign of Queen Victoria of the United Kingdom of Great Britain and Ireland—which lasted from 1837 until the Queen's death in 1901, the conventional wisdom was that females were by far the weaker sex and physical activity was not only unbecoming but

In response to criticism for encouraging his daughters to read and think, Samuel Blackwell would reply that his daughters were as capable of thinking as his sons were.

actually dangerous for their delicate constitutions. Moreover, education for females was frowned upon because it might fill girls' and women's minds with upsetting ideas and distract them from expected roles as wives, mothers, and helpmates to their husbands, whose right and duty it was to make their mark in the world.

Samuel Blackwell had no patience for this thinking. He wanted his daughters to have the same educational opportunities as his sons, the same exposure to healthful, vigorous exercise, the same chance to grow into fully actualized, productive adults. At least once a day, Blackwell required the governess to take the children on long walks around Bristol and into the countryside. He also had tutors for both his sons and daughters. In response to criticism for encouraging his daughters to read and think, he would reply that his daughters were as capable of thinking as his sons were.

UNREST IN BRISTOL

In the late 1820's, the family was reasonably prosperous. They kept a home in Bristol next to Samuel's sugar refinery and rented a charming cottage 9 miles (14 kilometers) away in

Olveston, where the family stayed during the summers. Samuel traveled to work every day in a carriage drawn by his horse, Bessie Gray, named after one of his daughters. But many other British citizens did not share this comfortable lifestyle. Poorhouses were crowded, and laws allowed factory and mine owners to employ poor women and children under horrible conditions for little or no wages. By the early 1830's, unstable social conditions gripped the country, and many people were angry and unhappy.

These conditions led to riots throughout England. Unrest erupted in Bristol in October 1831. For three days, mobs rioted in the city, setting fires and burning many buildings. Blackwell's sugar refinery survived the rioting. But there were growing financial concerns within the family. Blackwell's brother James had recently run Blackwell's business in Ireland into ruin. The failure of two sugar-importing businesses cost Samuel close to 70,000 pounds (about $7 million today), a fortune in those days. He knew it was time for a change, and he made the decision to move his family to the United States.

Blackwell was a valued and respected member of the Bristol community. Business leaders in the city pledged to lend him, at a very low interest rate, as much money as he might need to recover. But he declined the offer. He was determined to start anew in the United States, where his religious beliefs would not be cause for discrimination against him and where the sugar-refining innovations he had developed might prove profitable. Finally, he hoped that in America, he could begin to refine sugar from sugar beets instead of sugar cane, and detach his livelihood from slavery.

SAILING FOR AMERICA

Over the next few weeks, the Blackwells sold nearly all their belongings, deciding to take with them only a few cherished items, including their best china. The family, including the aunts, set sail for New York on a ship called the *Cosmo* in August 1832.

Elizabeth suffered terribly from seasickness throughout the voyage. The family's cabins in the back of the ship pitched and rolled violently and the windows leaked. Worst of all for Elizabeth and Anna, the ship's sewage drainpipe passed directly through their cabin. Anna wrote, "This hideous pillar leaked incessantly, despite the patchings and mendings of the ship-carpenter. What a dreadful experience was our 7 weeks and four days of misery in that floating hell!"[2] Elizabeth recounted in her autobiography years later that several passengers died of cholera during the trip. But the Blackwells avoided serious illness throughout the voyage and arrived in New York City healthy.

Chapter 2: Hardship on the Hudson, Misery on the Ohio

Within two weeks of their arrival in New York, the family rented a tall, narrow rowhouse on Thompson Street, near what is now Washington Square. Shortly after their arrival, the ninth Blackwell child, a son who was named George Washington, was born.

Blackwell wasted no time in setting up a sugar business. He introduced to the U.S. sugar industry his new method of sugar refining, called the vacuum pan process, which required less heat to crystallize the sugar syrup. Around 1835, he took over management of the Congress Sugar Refinery on Duane Street, which was owned by a London company called Gower, Guppy & Company. The vacuum pan process was successful and Blackwell worked hard to establish the business.

Life was good for the Blackwells for the first few years in New York. The Blackwell children explored the city. Elizabeth and her brother Sam especially enjoyed walking together while they discussed the books they were reading and the increasingly lofty ideas that were filling their young minds. The Blackwell children took French and music lessons; attended school and church; sang, danced, and played musical instruments; enjoyed plays and concerts; and in the winter went ice skating and sleigh riding.

WORKING FOR ABOLITION

As soon as the Blackwells got settled in New York, they began to associate with leading *abolitionists* (people who favored the compulsory abolition of Negro slavery). They often went to a Presbyterian church led by Samuel Hanson Cox.

Not long after their arrival in New York, Blackwell met a journalist who was beginning to gain fame as an abolitionist reformer. William Lloyd Garrison had founded the antislavery newspaper *The Liberator* in Boston in 1831, and one of the first abolitionist societies in 1832. He also was a leader in the American Anti-Slavery Society.

Blackwell met Garrison at an antislavery meeting in New York, and soon Garrison became a frequent guest in the Blackwell home, where Elizabeth listened to him talk about the horrors of slavery.

At abolitionist meetings, Elizabeth heard about a young teacher in Connecticut named Prudence Crandall, who had founded a school for African American girls and had been attacked by people opposed to her views and activities. Elizabeth was greatly impressed with Crandall and closely watched her struggles.

In 1834, Blackwell moved his family to a big frame house on Long Island near Newton, surrounded by gardens, an orchard, pastures, woods, and clover fields. The move was a happy one for Elizabeth, but ultimately may have proved deadly for Blackwell. A marsh next to the property was infested with mosquitoes, and Blackwell became ill with a disease that may have been malaria, which is transmitted to humans by mosquitoes.

Elizabeth's father, however, recovered from his illness for a while, and the family's home became a haven for abolitionists in need of a safe place to hide. One Sunday in 1834, Dr. Cox, the Presbyterian minister, preached a sermon in which he said that Jesus, as a Semite—one of a group of people who originally inhabited the regions of East Africa, North Africa, the Arabian Peninsula, and surrounding areas—surely had darker skin than the members of the congregation. Word quickly spread that Cox had declared that Jesus was a black man. A mob attacked his church and threatened to lynch the minister. Cox fled with his family to the Blackwell home.

The Blackwells did not live in this house long, however. By early 1835, they had moved to Paulus Hook—now known as Jersey City—to a big house overlooking the Hudson River with a magnificent view of the river traffic and the city. This house also became a center for antislavery activities. They hid a runaway slave at the house for several weeks while they made arrangements for her to travel to another country.

In 1834, abolitionist Dr. Samuel Hanson Cox, the Blackwell family physician and a Presbyterian minister whose church the family attended, preached a sermon in which he proclaimed that Jesus was a dark-skinned man. A mob attacked his church and threatened to lynch Cox, shown below. He fled with his family and took refuge at the Blackwell home.

A great fire broke out in New York City in December 1835. The fire spared Samuel Blackwell's sugar refineries, but insurance companies failed as a result of the huge claims from the fire, and Samuel's refineries were left without insurance coverage.

Elizabeth often accompanied her older sisters, Marian and Anna, when they attended antislavery fairs in New York City. Elizabeth's diary records an array of abolitionist organizations she took part in, including the Abolitionist Vigilance Committee, the Anti-Slavery Working Society, the Ladies Anti-Slavery Society, and the New York Anti-Slavery Society. After attending a young men's Anti-Slavery meeting in 1837, she was impressed by the speaker's observation that "you benefit yourself as well as the slave by interesting your sympathies in behalf of the oppressed, and that your treatment of the helpless bleeding victim before you, naked human nature stripped of every adventitious circumstance was a sure touchstone of your heart. . . ."[1]

FINANCIAL WOES

Meanwhile, Blackwell's business activities began to take a turn for the worse. He suffered greatly from a huge fire in New York City in December 1835. From their vantage point in Paulus Hook, the Blackwell family watched the distant flames. Samuel rushed out to look after the refinery. He returned three days later, when the flames were finally extinguished, with good news—his sugar refineries had survived the fire. But 40 square blocks of the city had been completely destroyed and many businesses were ruined. As a result of huge claims, insurance companies failed, and Samuel's refineries were left without insurance coverage. Fire was always a big danger at sugar refineries because the process required furnaces to burn continuously. Blackwell began to spend the night at the Congress refinery several times a week. But his efforts were futile. In late September of 1836, the refinery burned down. Gower, Guppy & Company decided not to rebuild. Blackwell bought another refinery, on Washington Street, and kept up the same vigil there. But by now his financial position was so unstable that he was forced to sell the business only six months later.

Perhaps it was a combination of her father's financial difficulties and her growing social activism that prompted Elizabeth to consider deeply her future and how she might find meaningful work. She realized that, as a woman, her options were strictly limited. Still, she dared hope. In 1838, she wrote, "How I do long for some end to act for some end to be obtained in this life, . . . to go on everyday in just the same jog trot manner without any object is very wearisome."[2]

Now Blackwell's business situation was so bad it began to have a direct effect on the family. From the comfortable upper-middle class life they had enjoyed in England, they now had been reduced to near poverty. In March 1838, Elizabeth wrote, "We are become so poor that [Papa] has put us upon an economical plan, we had no meat for dinner yesterday, today we had a stew composed of potatoes with a few bones which had been carefully preserved, and *one penny leek.*"[3]

An economic depression had descended on the United States in the late 1830's; many businesses collapsed. No one knows whether Blackwell could have weathered the financial storms that were driving his businesses into the ground. But his conscience was constantly at war with his business. As long as the raw material of his livelihood—sugar cane—was produced with slave labor, he never put his whole heart into it. Instead, he focused his hopes on developing a market for beet sugar. He enlisted Anna's help in translating books in French on the production of beet sugar and conducted mysterious experiments in the basement, which he never explained to the family.

The family's financial situation became so desperate by September 1837 that they had to take in paying boarders. Early in 1838, Blackwell, inspired by reports of unlimited business opportunities on the frontier—which at that time was anything west of New York—went on a fact-finding expedition to Ohio. When he returned he announced that the family would move to Cincinnati.

OHIO BOUND

The family sold some possessions, packed, and on May 3, 1838, boarded a boat to Philadelphia. Several members of the family stayed behind. Anna was teaching in Vermont, Marian was teaching in Manhattan, and Aunt Barbara and Aunt Lucy were running a millinery business in New York City.

From Philadelphia the Blackwells traveled by train to Columbia, Pennsylvania. A canal boat conveyed them from Columbia to Pittsburgh on the Pennsylvania Main Line Canal, and they continued by water routes to Hollidaysburgh, Pennsylvania. From there, they would begin their trip across the Allegheny Mountains.

They traveled on what was known as the Portage Railroad, which was not a railroad in the conventional sense, but a series of cars riding on tracks up the steep planes of the mountains. A stationary steam engine pulled the cars up the inclined planes on ropes. The Blackwells traveled by boat and railroad for several more days, finally reaching Cincinnati on May 12. Elizabeth wrote that she was "pleased with the appearance of the city,"[4] its new buildings, the surrounding hills, its cleanliness, and the bustling river traffic.

Within days of arriving, Blackwell leased a mill where he could refine sugar using water power. But the economic depression was affecting the frontier too. Business was bad, and he could not find a single person interested in his plan for producing beet sugar.

The Blackwells settled into life in Cincinnati. Blackwell rented a house on a hill overlooking the Ohio River. The family joined a church led by the abolitionist Lyman Beecher, who was the father of Harriet Beecher Stowe, author of the antislavery classic *Uncle Tom's Cabin*. Elizabeth gave music lessons. The family attended abolitionist meetings.

TRAGEDY, HARDSHIP, AND INDEPENDENCE

The illness—probably malaria—that Blackwell had caught when living on Long Island returned. In July 1838, he had begun to suffer spells of fainting. After that, he declined quickly. By August 3, the doctor declared Blackwell was near death. Elizabeth and her mother watched over him, but there was little they could do. On August 7, he died. Elizabeth wrote: "At 10 minutes past 10 he expired, . . . horrified I put my hand to his mouth and never till my dying day shall I forget the dreadful feeling when I found there was no breath it seemed so cold, then indeed we might weep without restraint and as I laid my hand on his still warm forehead what a feeling of hopeless despondency came over me."[5] Elizabeth felt that all hope and joy had gone out of her life.

If Elizabeth, then 17, and the family thought life had been hard during the past few years, they were soon to learn just how much more difficult it could become. An examination of Blackwell's business records revealed that he had left the family only $20 (about $380 today) in cash and was deeply in debt to his former partner Guppy. The family had to find a way to make money—fast. Before the month was over, the family had opened a little school in their home. They had only a few students. They called their school the Cincinnati English and French Academy for Girls, and it had day students as well as boarders. The curriculum included reading, writing, drawing, arithmetic, grammar, history, geography, philosophy, botany, French, and vocal music. Lessons in various musical instruments were also available.

In 1838, the Blackwells moved to Cincinnati, where they joined a church led by the abolitionist Lyman Beecher, shown above. Beecher was the father of Harriet Beecher Stowe, author of the famous antislavery novel Uncle Tom's Cabin.

American Transcendentalist Ralph Waldo Emerson, shown above, had a great impact on the young Elizabeth Blackwell.

But death returned to the Blackwell family. Aunt Mary fell sick, with what appeared to be the same illness that had taken her brother less than two months earlier, and in late September she died. In November, news came to them from New York: Aunt Barbara had died as well. Elizabeth, too numbed with grief over the death of her beloved father, observed mildly, "How strange it seems, one after the other."[6]

SPIRITUAL QUEST

Now that they were business owners, the Blackwell women found themselves forced to be more discrete about their antislavery leanings. Though Ohio was a free state, proslavery sentiment was not uncommon in Cincinnati. The women's humanitarian concerns found a safer outlet in the church. Elizabeth's mother, Hannah, joined a Presbyterian church, while Elizabeth, Anna, and Marian found themselves more comfortable with Episcopalianism. Elizabeth joined the denomination and taught in the Sunday school.

But Elizabeth and her two older sisters were constantly searching for a theology that made sense to them in their lives, and reflected the newest thinking in social and spiritual matters. Two years after Elizabeth became an Episcopalian, Elizabeth, Anna, and Marian joined a Unitarian church led by William Henry Channing, an outspoken abolitionist. There they were also introduced to Transcendentalism, a philosophy that stressed the power of the individual and claimed that the solution to human problems lies in the free development of individual emotions. The Transcendentalists emphasized self-reliance and individuality and said that individuals should reject the authority of Christianity and gain knowledge of God through reason. Elizabeth was quite taken with the young Reverend Channing. "I well remember the glowing face with which I found Mr. Channing reading a book just received," she wrote. "'Sit down,' he cried, 'and listen to this!'

and forthwith he poured forth extracts from Emerson's essays."[7] Elizabeth was deeply affected by the words of Ralph Waldo Emerson, the leading American Transcendentalist.

At the same time she was forging a personal faith and philosophy, Elizabeth's interest in the question of women's rights, which had first appeared in her writings as a young teen-ager, was deepening. She was filled with indignation after hearing a Roman Catholic bishop speak at a conference in which he expressed his opposition to the education of women.

Elizabeth soon would have the chance to strike out on her own, and to put her courage and beliefs to the test. Once again, in 1841, economic problems swept across the United States. It was the end for the Cincinnati English and French Academy for Girls. The school had been losing pupils for various reasons, not the least of which was the Blackwells' abolitionist beliefs. Proslavery forces within the Unitarian Church had forced Channing to resign as pastor. Many of the Blackwells' pupils, well aware of their connection to Channing, quit the school. It was forced to close its doors in 1842.

For the next few years, the older children of the Blackwell family pitched in to support the family. They took in boarders, who were cared for by Hannah, Marian, and Emily. Elizabeth tutored. Anna got a teaching job. Sam worked as a clerk, then a bookkeeper, while Henry became a traveling salesman. Then in 1844, an offer arrived at the Blackwell home. The town of Henderson, Kentucky, needed a girls' school. Would Anna, Marian, or Elizabeth be interested in setting one up? Elizabeth agreed to take the job. In March, Elizabeth, now 23, boarded a steamboat called the *Chieftain,* to take her down the Ohio River.

LONELY SCHOOLMISTRESS

Upon her arrival, she found "three dirty old frame buildings, a steep bank covered with mud, some negroes and dirty white people at the foot . . ."[8] Believing she would be boarding with a Henderson family, the Wilsons, the travel-weary Elizabeth asked to be shown upstairs. The Wilsons' young daughter obliged and Elizabeth was horrified to find herself in a room of unbearable shabbiness: "A little window looking upon the side of a house not two yards [1.8 meters] from it, the rough board walls daubed with old whitewash, the bed, the furniture, dirty, covered with litter and dust, all gloomy and wretched."[9] With some relief she found that this was not the room in which she would be living. Her lodgings would be with a different family who lived in a large, clean brick house.

But she was in for another shock when she announced to her hosts that she expected to begin teaching the following Monday, in three days. This would not be possible, they replied with alarm. They had just chosen the building that was to serve as a school and it was in disrepair—the plaster falling, the windows broken. Trustees had yet to been named. Still, Elizabeth told him firmly, she expected to begin teaching on Monday. By means of a combination of cool reason, stubborn insistence, good-natured encouragement, and forceful argument, the building was hastily cleaned up and the students were notified.

She almost met her goal—her first day of teaching was Tuesday, not Monday. She was in charge of 14 quiet, well-behaved girls. For three days a week she taught for 10 hours, the other four days she had little to do but socialize with the locals. Enduring endless visits with the overly friendly townspeople was wearisome to Elizabeth. She had nothing in common with them. The brisk walks that Elizabeth found invigorating were distasteful in the extreme to the pampered and listless young ladies. The conversation was unremittingly dull. "Carlyle's name," she exclaimed in a letter home, referring to the contemporary Scottish social philosopher Thomas Carlyle, "has never even been distantly echoed here, Emerson is a perfect stranger, and Channing, I presume, would produce a universal fainting-fit!"[10] She longed for a kindred spirit, some intelligent conversation, but nothing of the type was to be had. Lacking those, she craved solitude. But she was constantly surrounded by people with whom she shared nothing. "I do long to get hold of someone to whom I can talk frankly; this constant smiling and bowing and wearing a mask provokes me intolerably; it sends me internally to the other extreme, and I shall soon, I think, rush into the woods, vilify Henderson, . . ."[11]

She could not relate to the people her own age. One of their favorite summer pastimes was gathering in small groups on the riverbank, a place known as Lovers' Grove. She accompanied some young people there on a couple of occasions, but one time she found she had just had enough of their prattling. Without a word to her companions, she walked home alone. Later, when they asked her why she had left, she made fun of their "sentimental doings."[12] It was the last time she was invited to Lovers' Grove.

Elizabeth also shunned the more deliberate attentions of some of the young men of Henderson. "There are two rather eligible young males here, whose mothers have for some time been electioneering for wives; one tall, the other short, with very pretty names, of good family and with tolerable fortune, but unfortunately one seems to me a dolt, the other, well, not wise, so I keep them at a respectful distance, which you know I am quite capable of doing."[13]

Perhaps worst of all, though, was that she had to live in an environment in which slavery was a way of life, and everything she saw of it more than affirmed her belief that it was one of the world's supreme evils. Once Elizabeth was sitting on the porch with the woman in whose home she lived when a shabby, forlorn-looking slave who worked on the family's tobacco plantation approached his mistress to ask her for a clean shirt. At the same time, the lady's cool, elegantly dressed daughter appeared on the porch. The lady's response was to send the man away with harsh words. The experience upset Elizabeth deeply. She recalled in her autobiography: "The contrast of the two figures, the young lady and the slave, and the sharp reprimand with which his mistress from her rocking-chair drove the slave away, left a profound impression on my mind."[14]

In a letter from Henderson she wrote: "I dislike slavery more and more every day; I suppose I see it here in its mildest form, and since my residence here I have heard of no use being made of the whipping-post, nor any instance of downright cruelty. . . . But to live in the midst of beings degraded to the utmost in body and mind, drudging on from earliest morning to latest night, cuffed about by everyone, scolded at all day long, blamed unjustly, and without spirit enough to reply, with no consideration in any way for their feelings, with no hope for the future . . .to live in their midst, utterly unable to help them, is to me dreadful, and what I would not do long for any consideration. Meanwhile I treat them civilly, and dispense with their services as much as possible, for which I believe the poor creatures despise me."[15]

It was altogether too much for Elizabeth to bear. Henderson was a misery for Elizabeth in almost every way, physically, morally, socially. At the end of the first term in August, she quit. With much relief and probably wiser in the ways of the world and with a deeper conviction and a keener sense of self-knowledge, perhaps even more determined to find a satisfying career, she gratefully returned to Cincinnati.

Chapter 3: A Calling

While Elizabeth Blackwell had been in Henderson, Kentucky, her family had moved to Walnut Hills, a suburb of Cincinnati and home of Lane Theological Seminary. Their old acquaintance Lyman Beecher was a professor there, and Elizabeth renewed her friendship with his daughter Harriet, who inspired her with her ability to run a household full of boisterous and demanding children and also find time to pursue her passion—writing.

Harriet Beecher Stowe was probably the best—perhaps the only—example Blackwell had ever encountered of a woman who could combine marriage and career. Since they had been teen-agers, Blackwell and her sisters evaluated their prospects for marriage and the realities of married life, and found them to be uninspiring, if not downright distasteful. Even in their childhood, their grandmother Blackwell had warned them against marriage, describing it as servitude. Indeed, in the early 1800's, marriage essentially made women legal nonentities. The laws of most states made any money earned by a wife the property of her husband. A wife could not make her own will nor enter into a contract. She could not sue in court, or be sued. Most men, and many women as well, were more than content with this status quo, believing that it was the role of men to take care of all worldly concerns, leaving women, who were considered weaker in body, mind, and spirit, to be loving, devoted mothers and helpmates to their husbands. Women were the guardians of piety, morality, and virtue, but only from the protected and refined confines of the home. It was not a lifestyle that appealed to any of the Blackwell women. None of the Blackwell daughters ever married.

This did not stop Blackwell from falling in love when she returned to Cincinnati from Henderson. She joined a social organization called the Semi-Colon Club, which held weekly meetings that included literary readings and discussions followed by dinner and dancing. Her circle of friends there included prominent citizens, thinkers, and writers. Among this group was a young man with whom she developed a special relationship. He was cultured and highly educated, and attended many of the same club meetings and lectures.

But before long, it became clear to Blackwell that this man's progressive thinking did not extend to his expectations of a woman's role. Unwilling to enter into a marriage in which she would not be able to express her own ideas and views, she knew there was no future with him.

This romantic disappointment coincided with the illness of a family friend named Mary Donaldson. She was dying of a painful disease, most likely uterine cancer. Seeing her friend, pale and emaciated, must have been especially difficult for Blackwell, who was squeamish about the body and hated illness perhaps as much as she hated social injustice. But her friend had a special message for her. She told her of her embarrassment and discomfort to be treated for her distinctly female disease by a male doctor. She said her suffering would have been much less if she could have been cared for by a woman doctor. Then she noted how intelligent Elizabeth was and how much she liked to study. She asked Elizabeth why didn't she become a doctor. Elizabeth was taken aback. "I could not bear the sight of a medical book,"[1] she said. She was much more interested in history and metaphysics than in anything to do with the body.

But the idea of medicine took hold of her mind. Maybe this was the answer for her: a way of living an independent life, supporting herself in a career of which she could be proud and that would allow her to make a tangible difference in people's lives—a path that would spare her from the yoke of matrimony. Many years later, she wrote the following passage in an early draft of her autobiography:

> At this very time when the medical career was suggested to me I was experiencing an unusually strong struggle between attraction towards a highly educated man with whom I had been very intimately thrown, and the distinct perception that his views were too narrow and rigid, to allow of any close and ennobling companionship.
>
> I grew indignant with myself, a struggle that weakened me, and resolved to take a step that I hoped might cut the knot I could not

untie, and so recover full mental freedom! I finally made up my mind to devote myself to medical study, with the belief that I should thus place an insuperable barrier between myself and those disturbing influences, which I could not wisely yield to, but could not otherwise stifle. I long retained a bunch of flowers which had passed between us, done up in a packet which I sentimentally but in all sincerity labelled—young love's last dream.

I look back now, with real pity, at the inexperience of that enthusiastic young girl, who thus hoped to stifle the master passion of human existence.[2]

It appears that only after the passing of many years, did Elizabeth Blackwell fully comprehend what she had sacrificed.

"MORAL QUALITIES OF CHARACTER"

But Elizabeth was not quite ready to make a commitment to pursuing medicine—after all, it was the 1840's. What did it mean for a woman to consider such a career? It was literally almost unthinkable. Only a few occupations were open to women during this time. They could be teachers, like Blackwell and her sisters had been; they could be milliners, like her aunts Barbara and Lucy. Women were employed in factories, such as textile mills. They cleaned the houses, washed the laundry, and cared for the children of the wealthy. They also operated or worked in small businesses, running their own shops or taverns. Those lucky enough to have the talent and education could even be writers. But work that required advanced education was steadfastly denied to women.

The reasons for this were intimately woven into the fabric of the society of the 1800's. The "idealization" of women placed them far above men in the areas of spirituality, virtue, piety, and morality. At the same time, it meant that any job that might not harmonize with these valued qualities was seen as a threat to women. Women were seen as the influence that softened and civilized men, who, without them would be brutes. To allow women to participate in masculine professions, many people believed, would cause harm to both sexes.

Nowhere would this be more dangerous than in the practice of medicine. A Boston physician wrote in 1820 that women should not even be allowed to practice midwifery, the assistance of other women in childbirth. He believed that medical training and practice, which included such "ghastly" activities as dissection and surgery, required both mental toughness and a subduing of feelings of sympathy and compassion. Men could retain their humanity in the face of such horrors, but women's "refined sensibility"[3] would be crushed, their hearts hardened. He wrote: "A female could scarce pass through the course of education requisite to prepare her, as she ought to be prepared, for the practice of midwifery, without destroying those moral qualities of character, which are essential to the office."[4] Combine these attitudes with the belief, shared by many people in the 1800's, that women were naturally inferior physically, intellectually, more impulsive, more passive, hysterical, and unable to do math, and anyone would be justifiably horrified at the thought of entrusting life and health to a female physician—in the highly unlikely event that a woman could even become a physician.

Blackwell's friends—though they hardly agreed with these views—well understood their power. Even Harriet Beecher Stowe could not at first give her encouragement. There were too many obstacles, she told Blackwell—getting the proper education would be almost impossible, considering the expense and the unlikelihood of any medical school accepting a woman. And even if she could get that far, who would accept a woman doctor?

However, Blackwell received encouragement from one of the prominent intellectuals in Cincinnati, James H. Perkins. He told her, "I do wish you would take the matter up, if you have the courage—and you have the courage, I know."[5] Elizabeth wrote in her autobiography, "So invigorating was his judgment, that I felt at the moment as if I could conquer the world."[6] She received a letter from Dr. Abraham Liddon Cox, the brother of the family's former physician in New York, Samuel Cox. Although he gave no words of encouragement, Dr. Cox gave her a list of medical schools. She chose to take this list as encouragement. Elizabeth Blackwell had made up her mind to pursue medicine.

MEDICAL STUDENT

Blackwell's first pressing problem was money. At that time, a medical education cost about $3,000 (about $62,000 today), a huge sum, considering that she had earned $400 (about $8,300 today) for teaching in Henderson. She also knew she was deficient in certain subjects, notably science, Greek, and Latin, which she would need to pursue her medical studies.

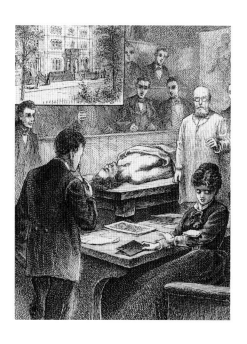

An opportunity to fill both her financial and educational gaps arose in the form of a teaching position in Asheville, North Carolina. The school was run by a former doctor and now Presbyterian minister named John Dickson. Elizabeth would earn $250 (about $5,200 today) a year for every 10 students she taught, plus room and board. And Dickson would guide her in introductory medical studies.

Blackwell is depicted as a medical student in this drawing of a scene in the operating room of a medical college.

Blackwell left for Asheville on June 16, 1845. Her brothers Sam and Howard escorted her. The 11-day journey by horse-drawn wagon over rutted roads and through magnificent countryside might have seemed long, but it was only the first step in her much longer and more difficult journey to a medical degree.

Asheville was a pleasant surprise for Elizabeth after the disappointment of Henderson. Her first sight of the town, "entirely surrounded by the Alleghenies, a beautiful plateau, through which the rapid French Broad River ran,"[7] pleased her. She found the Dicksons to be cultured, welcoming, and supportive; her room in their house had windows with lovely views of the village and the surrounding hills; and the school was pleasant.

But the realization of the challenge that lay ahead, and the security and familiarity she was leaving behind soon overwhelmed her. A few days after their arrival, it was time for Sam and Howard to leave. After their goodbyes, she recalled some months later in a letter to her brother Henry, she retreated to her room and looked at the nighttime vista. She was filled with doubt and dread of what lay before her. She called out to God for guidance and support.

"Suddenly, overwhelmingly," she wrote, "an answer came. A glorious presence, as of brilliant light, flooded my soul. There was nothing visible to the physical sense; but a spiritual influence so joyful, gentle, but powerful, surrounded me that the despair which had overwhelmed me vanished. All doubt as to the future, all hesitation as to the rightfulness of my purpose, left me, and never in afterlife returned. I *knew* that, however insignificant my individual effort might be, it was in a right direction, and in accordance with the great providential ordering of our race's progress."[8]

Blackwell's work and social life were satisfying. The Dicksons' circle of friends were educated people who enjoyed discussing the great ideas of the day. Dickson gave her access to the medical books in his library, including *Popular Medicine, Oliver's First Lines of Physiology: Designed for the Use of Students of Medicine,* and *Pereira's A Treatise on Food and Diet.* She read diligently.

In Asheville, Blackwell experienced two small, but important, firsts in her medical journey, her first dissection and her first cure. The former was performed on a large, dead beetle presented to her by a fellow teacher. This was just the kind of encounter that filled Blackwell with revulsion. Years earlier at school in New York, the teacher brought to class a calf's eyeball. One glance at the glistening orb nestled in gobs of bloody fat had repelled her.

Now she was faced with the prospect of handling the corpse of a loathsome insect. Equipped with a penknife and a hairpin, she hovered over the dead insect for some time, gathering her nerve. Finally she cut into it. The dessicated beetle yielded nothing but a pinch of yellowish dust. But the experience yielded much more—courage. Never again would she be afraid of dissection.

Blackwell's first cure was effected on Mrs. O'Heara, an elderly friend of the Dickson family, who was suffering from a severe headache. Blackwell decided to try hypnotism on Mrs. O'Heara. "I offered to relieve her, half doubting my own powers, never having attempted anything of the kind," she recalled. "In a quarter or half an hour she was entirely relieved and declared some good angel sent me to her aid."[9] The cure earned her the title "Dr. Blackwell" in the Dickson household.

Chapter 4: A Moral and Professional Crusade

Slavery continued to occupy Blackwell's mind. The Reverend Dickson claimed to be an abolitionist; nevertheless, he owned slaves. Blackwell and Dickson's wife joined forces to plan a school where they would teach slaves to read. Because this was against the law, Dickson would not give his permission. But he agreed to let them give the slaves oral bible instruction. So in July, Elizabeth and Mrs. Dickson opened a Sunday school for slaves, with five teachers, all but Elizabeth slaveowners, and 25 students. Blackwell was troubled by the hypocrisy of slaveowners teaching Christianity while, in her eyes, violating its teachings drastically. She also despaired at the tedium of the lessons and the mediocrity of the teachers' thinking, and struggled with her own involvement in the institution of slavery. In a letter to her mother, Blackwell wrote: "I sometimes reproach myself for my prudence, and the calmness with which I answer some outrageous injustice while I'm really raging with indignation—but it is the only way, in which I can hope to do any good, for the slightest display of feeling arms all their prejudices, and I am no orator to convert by a burst of passionate eloquence, so I must ever go on in my own quiet manner, knowing that it does not proceed from cowardice."[1] This sensitivity to prevailing attitudes and lack of illusion about her ability to influence them would serve her well later on as she made her way through medical school as a lone woman.

The local authorities soon got wind of the slave school and shut it down. Dickson's school was struggling, too. Enrollment was down and Dickson's health declined. He closed the school in the winter of 1846.

Elizabeth traveled to the home of Dickson's brother, Samuel, who was a highly respected physician and medical professor in Charleston, South Carolina. She would be a guest in his home, he would help her with her medical studies, and she could find work in the city. This she did, spending the next year and a half studying Greek and reading books on anatomy and surgery. To earn money, she taught music for eight hours a day at a boarding school owned by a woman named Madame Du Pre—which she hated, complaining in a letter to her sister Marian that she was constantly annoyed by "dirty, disorderly rooms, & the constant society of noisy uneducated girls. . . ."[2]

Blackwell also diligently wrote letters, asking advice of every physician whose name was suggested to her. She corresponded with Friedrich A. Adler, a New York physician, who told her he would be willing to tutor her in obstetrics. She got qualified encouragement from a Quaker physician in Philadelphia named Joseph Warrington. He warned her, though, that none of his patients would ever consult a woman doctor and that, in his opinion, since women were meant to be men's helpmates, they should fill the role of nurses. Nevertheless, he offered to meet with her if she ever found herself in Philadelphia.

"It was, to my mind, a moral crusade on which I had entered, a course of justice and common sense, and it must be pursued in the light of day, and with public sanction, in order to accomplish its end."

Elizabeth Blackwell

With even this scant encouragement, she was not about to leave this opportunity to chance. In May 1847, she boldly embarked for Philadelphia, the center of American medicine at the time.

Another Quaker physician, William Elder, and his wife gave Blackwell a place to stay. She also met in person with Warrington, whom she easily won over and who allowed her to attend his lectures, go on patient rounds with him, and use his library. Dr. Jonathan M. Allen tutored her in anatomy. It was he who introduced her to her first human dissection—a wrist. She was enthralled. In her autobiography she wrote, "The beauty of the tendons and exquisite arrangements of this part of the body struck my artistic sense, and appealed to the sentiment of reverence with which this anatomical branch of study was ever afterwards invested in my mind."[3]

In Philadelphia, Blackwell consulted with a number of physicians about the possibility of entering a medical school. She also started actively applying to schools in Philadelphia and New York

City. She quickly learned of the many objections to a female studying or practicing medicine. Most of the men who made admissions decisions were firmly against admitting women to their programs. She was getting used to hearing the platitudes about women's intellectual inferiority, physical delicacy, and emotional susceptibility. But another attitude—professional rivalry—stood between Blackwell and her goal. The male doctors who were willing to consider that women were qualified to join them in their profession did not want to share opportunities with women. They feared they would lose patients to female doctors. As Blackwell recounted in her diary: "The fear of successful rivalry which at that time often existed in the medical mind was expressed by the dean of one of the smaller schools, who frankly replied to the application, 'You cannot expect us to furnish you with a stick to break our heads with'; so revolutionary seemed the attempt of a woman to leave a subordinate position and seek to obtain a complete medical education."[4]

Blackwell rejected suggestions by sympathetic physicians that she study in Paris, or that she attend medical school disguised as a man. To her, getting a medical education was linked with her dearly held conviction that women had the same right to it as did men. "It was, to my mind, a moral crusade on which I had entered, a course of justice and common sense, and it must be pursued in the light of day, and with public sanction, in order to accomplish its end."[5]

MAKING A STIR

After being rejected by all the New York and Philadelphia medical schools, Blackwell approached the smaller, so-called country schools in the region, applying to the 12 best. She also took a trip out East, visiting Anna and other relatives. In late October, she received a letter from one of these country schools. Geneva Medical College of Western New York was offering her admission. The letter implied that the Geneva faculty had reacted to her application favorably, but that they felt that they could only admit her with the approval of the all-male student body. The result of this consultation was outlined in a document included with the letter. It read:

> At a meeting of the entire medical class of Geneva Medical College, held this day, October 20, 1847, the following resolutions were unanimously adopted:—
>
> 1. Resolved—*That one of the radical principles of a Republican Government is the universal education of both sexes; that to every branch of scientific education the door should be open equally to all; that the application of Elizabeth Blackwell to become a member of our class meets our entire approbation; and in extending our unanimous invitation we pledge ourselves that no conduct of ours shall cause her to regret her attendance at this institution.*
>
> 2. Resolved—*That a copy of these proceedings be signed by the chairman and transmitted to Elizabeth Blackwell.*
>
> T. J. Stratton, Chairman.[6]

Blackwell could hardly know it at the time but a very different sentiment lurked under the idealism of these words. All she knew, or cared about, was that she was accepted to medical school, not one of the prestigious schools perhaps, but a fairly respectable one. She set off in haste for Geneva on November 4, already several weeks late for the start of the term.

The atmosphere at Geneva Medical College was not, as a rule, the epitome of academic discipline. The 150 young men who made up the student body tended to be rowdy pranksters, who often disrupted lectures with their shenanigans. Blackwell, ironically, owed her admission to the students' high-spirited irreverence. When Blackwell's application arrived, the faculty wanted to deny it unilaterally. But she was clearly qualified and they were reluctant to offend Dr. Warrington, who had sponsored her application. In a maneuver designed to shift the responsibility of her rejection to the students, they turned her application over to them to accept or deny as they saw fit. The faculty underestimated the students' capacity for turning pretty much anything into a joke. Their reaction to Blackwell's application was to erupt into pandemonium. They whooped and hollered, threw things, made outrageous speeches supporting her application, and finally called a vote. Every student but one loudly voted yes. The other students fell upon the single dissenter and he obligingly changed his vote.

Two weeks later, the arrival of Blackwell, a prim yet dignified and determined young woman in a plain dress and unadorned bonnet, stunned the dean and the students alike. They had never expected her to actually enroll. When she entered the lecture hall, which had only moments before been in the usual throes of unruliness, the students fell into a stunned but respectful silence, and stayed that way until the end of the lecture. The tiny lady perched in the front row, paying rapt attention to the instructor and taking careful notes, had a definite civilizing effect on the male students. The professors were kind as well, offering to help her catch up by lending her their notes or giving her private tutoring.

No such courtesy was offered to her in town, though. The people of Geneva were not ready to accept a female medical student in their community. The women of Geneva were steadfast in their indignation, gawking at her from a distance and haughtily sweeping their skirts aside when she passed them on the sidewalk. Her autobiography recounted: "I afterwards found that I had so shocked Geneva propriety that the theory was fully established either that I was a bad woman, whose designs would gradually become evident, or that, being insane, an outbreak of insanity would soon be apparent."[7]

Awaiting Blackwell was a much-dreaded meeting with Dr. James Webster, professor of anatomy. She had been warned that the professor was an unusual character and might not allow her to attend his lectures or dissections, both of which would have been a serious blow to her education. But the meeting turned out to be a happy surprise. Instead of the rejection she was led to expect, Webster greeted her with enthusiasm. What a great thing, he beamed, to have a woman medical student among them. He asked what subjects she had already studied. When she replied that she had studied everything but surgery, Webster was adamant. She absolutely must study surgery, he said. This "fat little fairy in the shape of the Professor of Anatomy,"[8] as she very affectionately described him, confirmed her determination to become a surgeon. Considering all the conditions requiring surgery that affected women, he observed, "Only think what a well-educated woman doctor would do in a city like New York. Why, she'd have her hands full in no time; her success would be immense. Yes, yes, you'll go through the course, and get your diploma with great *éclat* too; we'll give you all the opportunities. You'll make a stir, I can tell you."[9]

Her classmates tested her at first, tossing notes at her during lectures, all of which she pointedly ignored. The way she moved from lecture to lecture, with a cheerful, yet dignified manner, soon won over the student body, many of whom would become her lifelong friends.

In the larger world, however, her example was becoming an inspiration to some. Her activities were reported in newspapers along the East Coast. More women applied—or reapplied, if they had been rejected previously—to medical school.

The term ended and she easily passed her exams in January, whereupon she returned to Philadelphia. She had eight months to fill before her second term at Geneva would begin in October. Although professors had promised to write her letters of introduction, none had followed through, and no hospital would accept her for clinical training. In February, she received a letter of introduction that eventually secured her a position in the Blockley Almshouse. This place was a hospital designed to serve the poor people of Philadelphia. As such, it was poorly staffed, overcrowded, and underheated. But it would provide Blackwell with valuable insight into the plight of the poor, especially poor women.

FIRST CLINICAL EXPERIENCE

Blackwell was assigned a room in the women's syphilitic ward, where women suffering from the ravages of syphilis, a sexually transmitted disease, were treated. There, she was able to witness the effects of sexually transmitted diseases and gain insight into the social conditions that led to them. She saw young domestic servants who were forced into sexual relations by their employers and then thrown out of the house when they became ill. "All this is horrible!" she wrote. "Women must really open their eyes to it. I am convinced that they must regulate this matter. But how?"[10]

The male medical residents at Blockley, who were her own age, extended no gestures of friendship or support—quite the opposite. When she entered a room, they left it. When they noticed that she was reading the medical charts on the patients' beds, they stopped recording their diagnoses and treatments there. They even spied on her through the keyhole of her door at night, an activity she facilitated by deliberately placing her desk directly in the keyhole's sightline. Still, the experience, taken as a whole, was valuable to her professional development. The chief physician, Dr. Benedict, was so supportive and kind—overflowing with compassion for his dying and destitute patients—that Elizabeth described him to her mother as "the very loveliest man the Almighty ever created."[11] When a group of immigrants from Ireland suffering from typhus was admitted, she decided to do her graduation thesis on the disease. Typhus is a potentially deadly bacterial disease—though bacteria had not yet been identified as the causes of disease at that time—spread by the bites of such animals as lice, ticks, and fleas. Typhus outbreaks occur where there is overcrowding and poor sanitation, such as on ships.

She recorded all her observations on the disease and its treatment. Blackwell began to develop her own philosophy of the treatment of disease, which relied heavily on prevention. In a thesis based on her observations, she stressed the importance of cleanliness and personal hygiene in order to fight the disease. She wrote, "When the laws of health are generally understood and practised: when a social providence is extended over all ranks of the community, . . . —then we may hope to see these physical evils disappear, with all the moral evils which correspond to, and are constantly associated, with them."[12]

Sept. 22, 1848, was Blackwell's last day at Blockley. "How glad I am, to-morrow, to-morrow, I go home to my friends!"[13] she wrote in her journal. And it was an apt remark. In Geneva, her classmates welcomed her back warmly. In her journal she recorded that the "class seem so very friendly. One set me a chair, another spoke so pleasantly, and I had several little friendly chats. How little they know my sensitiveness to these trifling tokens!"[14] Not only did they accept her input into lively debates on all the controversial topics of

Blackwell is shown in a portrait done shortly after she became a doctor.

the day, including abolitionism, but they also continued to act decorously in her presence. Everyone had found a way to be cordial while maintaining the polite distance that was required between men and women at that time.

DOMINA

January 1849 marked the end of the term, and examinations were administered in mid-January. If Blackwell was nervous about her performance, she need not have been. In a letter to her sister Marian, she exclaimed, ". . . my face burned, my whole being was excited, but a great load was lifted from my mind."[15] She not only passed her finals with ease, but graduated first in her class.

On the day of the graduation ceremony, despite repeated urgings from Webster, Blackwell declined to march in the traditional procession through town with the other graduates, declaring the activity unladylike. Instead, she showed up at the Presbyterian church, the site of the ceremony, on the arm of her brother Henry. The sight that greeted her must have been a bit of a surprise, for the pews were filled with women—many of them the very same women of Geneva who had shunned her so thoroughly during her residence there. Henry recalled, "Of course when we came in there was a general stir and murmur, and everybody turned to look at us."[16]

The dean, Dr. Charles Lee, gave an address in which he named Blackwell as the head of the class. When the college's president handed out the diplomas, among all the dozens of times he uttered "*Domine,*" the Latin word for male doctor, came one "*Domina,*" for Elizabeth Blackwell, the first woman ever to earn the M.D. degree. After taking her diploma, Blackwell addressed the president. "Sir, I thank you. By the help of the Most High, it shall be the effort of my life to shed honor upon your diploma."[17] The audience applauded.

Blackwell's success was reported in foreign papers. The local newspaper described her in slightly patronizing terms, focusing more on her womanly charms and tenderness than on her momentous accomplishment: "She is good looking—a face that wins favorably upon you; affable in her manner she pleases you; intelligent and witty, she amuses you; amiable and confiding she wins upon you. . . . ELIZABETH BLACKWELL, the world cannot thank thee too much! God speed thee in thy work of mercy, and as an angel spirit to cherish and to soothe, mayst thou bend over the couch of the sick and the dying!"[18]

Armed with only a degree, Blackwell was hardly ready to start the fabulous practice that she had long desired. She needed more clinical experience. Though her success in medical school had softened attitudes toward women in medicine slightly, opportunities for clinical work were scant at best in the United States. Blackwell would have to travel to Paris. Not only did she hope Paris hospitals would be more open to women practitioners, but Paris was known throughout the world as a center of medical innovation.

Chapter 5: Losing Eyesight, Gaining Vision

Elizabeth Blackwell arrived in England on April 30, 1849. Her short stay there was filled with social engagements and professional activities. Through a friend of the family, she was introduced to a surgeon who invited her to observe a leg amputation. She watched the bloody and painful proceedings—at that time such operations were generally performed without anesthesia—with calm interest. She visited other hospitals in London and Birmingham. She went to party after party—"Engagement treads upon engagement, so that I've hardly a moment to think,"[1] she wrote—and even discovered that she had a taste for champagne.

LEARNING AT LA MATERNITÉ

Blackwell arrived in Paris in May. She found lodgings and was pleased at the chance to attend lectures, but she found that her American advisers' confidence at the ease with which she would find opportunities for clinical training were highly exaggerated. The Paris doctors Blackwell spoke with were every bit as dismissive of Blackwell, the female doctor, as had been any in America, barring her admission into their hospitals, or agreeing to admit her—if she were willing to disguise herself as a man. Firmly, she refused. She would get her training, as she had always done, openly, as a woman, or not at all.

Several doctors urged her to apply as a student at La Maternité, a maternity hospital, where young women were trained as midwives. Though La Maternité was a respected, world-famous facility, it was not an ideal situation for the young doctor. Most of the rest of the students were barely 20 years old, rowdy, uneducated country girls. Blackwell would not only have to perform the same duties as these girls but would have to live with them in a large dormitory room. But it was the only opportunity open to her.

On Blackwell's first night there, she helped deliver eight babies. She received a large apron, which she was warned would be replaced at her own expense if she lost it. The delivery room was large, dimly lit, and contained several beds. A fire burned on the hearth, and the room was equipped with a multitude of copper and tin utensils as well as tables and chairs. As they came into the world, each newborn was stashed on a large wooden stand in the center of the room. In the morning, the head midwife, Madame Charrier, appeared and the cloth covering the infants was whisked away, and the babies presented to her. The sight, Elizabeth wrote, "was really very droll. Each little shapeless red visage peeped from under a coarse peaked cap, on the front of which was a large label with the name and sex; a black serge jacket with a white handkerchief pinned across, and a small blanket tightly folded round the rest of the body, completed the appearance of the little mummy. . . ."[2]

The young French students, though far behind her in experience and education, were good-natured and for the most part eager to learn, and some of them gained Blackwell's admiration and affection. Of one she wrote: "I admire her vigorous life, I like to see her in the infirmary; she tends the sick with such an honest awkwardness, such a kind heart, and lifts them like babies in her strong arms, that I see the green fields and smell the sweet country air as I watch her."[3]

And Blackwell made a special friend, a handsome medical resident a couple of years her junior named Hippolyte Blot. Every week she watched him administer vaccinations, scratching the little arms of the squalling newborns with his knife. Soon, she began to notice a certain discomfort in his manner toward her. "He colours, or passes his hand through his hair and looks intently at the baby, in a very un-Frenchmanlike manner. I think he must be very *young*, or very much in awe of me, for he never ventures to give me a direct look, and seems so troubled when I address him that I very rarely disturb his life in that way."[4]

Soon he was loaning her medical texts and drawing her attention to interesting medical cases in the wards. Their friendly professional association blossomed soon after, when he asked her, somewhat awkwardly, if she would tutor him in English. They spent hours in the infirmary together, discussing the medical cases and new medical discoveries. They took long walks and enjoyed wide-ranging conversations.

In 1849, Blackwell sought graduate education as a student midwife at La Maternité, a maternity hospital in Paris.

Blackwell realized that she was falling in love. She agreed to stay on at La Maternité for an extra three months, to extend the term of her invaluable training, but also to spend more time in the company of her treasured friend.

While at La Maternité, Blackwell had the opportunity to witness the surgical removal of a large bladder stone from a female patient. This experience and other experiences at La Maternité cemented Blackwell's determination to become a surgeon.

Little did Blackwell know that in less than a month one tragic event would dash forever two of her most dearly held dreams.

A PHYSICAL SETBACK

In November, Blackwell had been caring for an infant with an eye infection that frequently caused blindness. One morning she was making her rounds in the dim early light. Stopping at the crib of this tiny patient, she noticed that its eyes were crusted shut. Bending low over the baby's face in the dim light, she syringed the infected fluid from the baby's eye, and a little bit of the fluid splashed up into her own left eye. She paid it little notice and completed her 12-hour shift. By that evening she knew something was wrong. Her eye felt scratchy. The next morning the eye was swollen and the lids were crusted shut. She ran to Blot. She had caught the terrible infection.

Blot cared for Blackwell personally during the next few critical days, administering every treatment available at the time. Her sister Anna, who was also living in Paris at the time, described her treatment in a letter to the family: "She has had little or no medicine, leeches once to the temple; ½ the forehead painted over, for a day or two, with mercury & hellebore; every hour the eye syringed with tepid water, externally and internally to wash out the immense quantity of matter constantly exuding; & every two hours M. Blot with fine pincers, peeled off the false membranes constantly forming over the globe."[5]

Blackwell lay for three weeks in the hospital, both eyes cauterized, but the damage was done. The sight in her left eye was gone. Thankfully, her right eye, which also had become infected, began to clear. As she prepared to leave the hospital, thankful for his unwavering care, she sent her friend Blot a gift of two lamps for his office.

But any hopes she might have had for a future at his side had been wiped out along with her vision. Later she recorded her private grief in her journal: ". . . how strongly my life turns to him, and yet that terrible suffering has put a distance between us that nothing can remove."[6]

Besides, Blackwell had always been somewhat insecure about her attractiveness to men, and she well understood the terrific difficulties that would arise if she tried to combine marriage with the career she envisioned for herself. Blot was delighted by her gift, and he came to her room at the hospital to thank her. He was, she wrote, "longing to be amiable, yet too conscientious to infringe the rules of the Maternité by acknowledging the present. He admired my braid of long hair, wondered how fingers without eyes could arrange anything so beautifully regular; spoke of the Protestant religion, thought if he joined any Church it would be that; turned to go, turned back again, and was evidently hardly able to leave without thanking me . . ."[7]

It seems there was an unspoken agreement between the two—despite the internal struggle—that their paths would take them away from each other. In a letter to her sister Emily she wrote, "I shall miss him exceedingly when I leave [Paris], for there is a most affectionate sympathy between us—but—a reformer's life is not a garden of roses."[8]

In the months following her release from the hospital, Blackwell stayed with Anna. She continued to hope, somewhat unreasonably, for the recovery of her left eye. She wrote to her uncle Charles: "In truth . . . the accident might have been so much worse that I am more disposed to rejoice than to complain. . . . As to the more serious consideration—loss of vision—I still hope to recover that in time, and meanwhile the right eye grows daily stronger. . . . I still mean to be at no very distant day *the first lady surgeon in the world.*"[9]

Blackwell was too weak to do much. She visited a few clinics and attended a few lectures, but found it difficult to concentrate. Blot visited her in the evenings to read to her. Still, it was not until early 1850—a few months after the accident—that she wrote a letter to her family. Her brother Sam recalled the contents of the letter in his diary. "She can distinguish the flame of a lamp as thro. thick mist and can discern something when the hand is passed across the eye. Her sense of the greatness of the loss is unspeakable—her calm endurance & patience for the remaining eye just such as might be expected from Elizabeth."[10]

Blackwell cousin Kenyon Blackwell made the rounds in London on her behalf, seeking a clinical appointment for her. He found one, at St. Bartholomew's Hospital, one of London's foremost medical facilities, where the eminent surgeon James Paget worked.

But before she returned to London, Blackwell traveled to Germany in June to try hydropathy, a medical therapy that was in vogue at the time. Practitioners of hydropathy used no drugs to treat illness. Instead, patients were treated by immersing them in baths, dousing them with showers, wrapping them in wet sheets, and compelling them to drink huge amounts of water. Blackwell reported no relief from this treatment. She complained instead that the "*abreibung* [rubdown] deadens my fingers, the sitz bath gives me the colic, the wet bandages impede digestion, & tonight I went to bed with quite a feverish attack, which gave me unpleasant dreams the whole night."[11]

After enduring only a few days of this treatment, Blackwell left Germany hardly cured—indeed, the infection in her left eye had flared up again. She returned to Paris, where a physician recommended that the left eye be removed to prevent it from infecting the right eye. This was done in August, and doctors installed a glass eye. The glass eye restored her appearance, and she could once again read. Her spirits lifted.

But now Blackwell had to accept the horrible fact that everyone close to her had known for a long time. Without full eyesight, her hopes of becoming a surgeon were forever extinguished. Anna broke the news to the family: "Elizabeth has suffered horribly. She has lost so much time, and will probably lose a good deal more before she can go on with her studies, and buoyed up she was to the last with the idea of regaining the sight of that eye (which everyone but herself knew a year ago to be quite out of the question). The certainty of its loss has been a terrible blow to her. It is indeed one of the saddest of all the many sad things I have seen in my lifetime."[12]

Though she would never be a surgeon, she was, after all, already a doctor. And in London, a clinical position at a large, renowned hospital awaited her. She left Paris and arrived in London in the middle of October.

CAREER REFOCUS

Blackwell spent about nine months in London at St. Bartholomew's and for the most part was accepted by the male students and faculty. She attended James Paget's lectures on *pathology* (the study of the causes and nature of diseases) and *physiology* (the science dealing with the normal functions of living things or their parts), she made the rounds of the wards, and investigated what would today be known as alternative medicine. She was dissatisfied with many of the practices of the conventional medicine of her day, but she also found much to be desired from the alternative methods. She wrote in a letter to her sister Emily, "It has been a heavy, perplexing subject to me on what system I should practise, for the old one appeared to me wrong, and I have thought every heresy better; but since I have been looking into these heresies a little more closely I feel as dissatisfied with them as with the old one."[13]

News of Blackwell's activities had spread among the more progressive women in Britain. One day, three of these women—Bessie Rayner Parkes, Barbara Leigh Smith, and Anna Smith—appeared at her room, offering her friendship. These women brought a cheerful lightness into her life and introduced her to prominent British scientists, authors, and politicians. These friends shared her interest in women's rights and her desire to make positive changes in society, and some of them were to remain her friends for the rest of her life.

One such friend was Florence Nightingale, a woman of about the same age as Blackwell from an extremely wealthy family. Nightingale would eventually earn lasting fame for her care of wounded soldiers in the Crimean War (1853–1856) and as the founder of the modern nursing profession. But when Bessie and Barbara introduced Blackwell and Nightingale in April 1851,

Blackwell discussed the possibility of opening a hospital in England with Florence Nightingale, the founder of the modern nursing profession. Nightingale gained fame for her care of wounded soldiers in the Crimean War, as shown in this 1856 illustration.

Nightingale was still living with her parents at their opulent estate, Embley Park in Hampshire, England. Blackwell and Nightingale spent much time together discussing the possibility of founding a hospital together at Embley. Nightingale, who had spent much time studying health reforms for the poor, impressed upon Blackwell the important relationship between hygiene and health. In Nightingale's view, human health was most imperiled by dirt, drink, diet, dampness, drafts, and drains. Though this philosophy may seem overly simplistic today, it was fairly astute—and valuable—medical thinking at a time when the relationship between germs and disease was not yet understood.

Blackwell's concern for the social and medical needs of women began to coalesce around the difficulties that befell women who were poorly educated in sexual matters. In a letter to a friend, she wrote, "The vast evils which result to society from the abuse of sex, in any way, should be concisely but powerfully taught. Mothers are so culpably ignorant and negligent in regard to this subject, that their attention should be firmly grasped, and facts laid before them which could not be forgotten—and clear information is absolutely necessary, that the remedies may be wisely chosen."[14]

Life in London also exposed Blackwell to the predicament of prostitutes, and she was able to build on the insights she gained while at Blockley Almshouse on the plight of poor women. She began to understand the toll that prostitution took on women and dreamed of a social movement to do away with this institution, an effort she called "a grand moral reform society, a great movement of women in this matter."[15]

By summer, Blackwell was faced with the decision about the next step in her career. Though she would have dearly liked to have settled permanently in London, she had no money to start a practice. The United States also seemed to offer more opportunities for a young female doctor. Within the past three years two medical colleges for women in Philadelphia and Boston had opened their doors. Besides, her younger sister Emily had decided to take up medicine as well, so she was further drawn homeward by the promise of a professional partner.

Chapter 6: Elizabeth Blackwell, M.D.

At the end of July 1851, Elizabeth set sail for New York. She was immediately met with prejudice because of her profession. Calling on a number of building owners, who had advertised space available for use as a doctor's office, she found none willing to rent to a "woman doctor." Neither Elizabeth's diploma nor credentials could overcome the prejudice that this term aroused, for "woman doctor" was the popular term for female *abortionist* (a doctor who performs a medical procedure to end pregnancy before birth). No respectable owner could afford to risk renting to a person performing such disreputable work. Finally, she found living quarters on University Place in a decent neighborhood, but she was forced to rent an entire floor at an inflated price. She announced the opening of her practice in the newspaper and waited for patients. Few came.

She lived in poverty, rationing food and coal for her stove. Her application for a position working at a large *dispensary* (free outpatient clinic) in the city was rejected. A few patients called, but other people sent her nasty letters. Her landlady refused to take messages for her.

Idle, alone, and lonely, Blackwell passed her first few months in New York writing letters to her family and to her supportive friends in England. In the meantime, Emily was applying to medical schools and, like her sister, was suffering rejection after rejection. Finally, Rush Medical College, in Chicago, accepted her as a student, and she started classes in the fall of 1852.

"LAWS OF LIFE"

In late 1851 or early 1852, Blackwell decided that a worthwhile way to fill her time would be to give lectures. In the 1800's, attending lectures was a popular pastime among middle-class women. Blackwell could make a little money, and perhaps market her medical practice. She began to write. Her topic was what would perhaps be known today as sex and health education for girls and women. She placed the following ad in the March 1, 1852 issue of the *New-York Daily Times*: "Dr. Elizabeth Blackwell will deliver a course of Lectures to ladies on the Laws of Life, with special reference to the Physical Education of Girls. The lectures will commence on Monday, March 1st, at 2 o'clock P.M. Tickets to the course $2, For sale at Evans & Brittan's Bookstore only, No. 697 Broadway."[1]

The course would consist of a series of lectures, to be delivered in a church basement. Her audience consisted largely of well-educated Quaker women, and she regaled them in clear yet sometimes poetically romanticized language with her philosophy of healthy living for females—physical, emotional, intellectual, and spiritual. She criticized many of the faults that she believed led to bad health and ultimately unhappiness—among them lack of exercise, idleness, poor diet, and lack of intellectual stimulation.

The remedy sounded fairly simple, consisting of her "Laws of Life": exercise, living in an orderly fashion, blending the life of the soul with that of the body, and using the body for the highest possible purposes. Blackwell described a set of accomplishments a girl should have achieved by the time she was a teen-ager: "By the age of 16 or 17," Blackwell preached, "under proper training, she would have acquired a strong, graceful and perfectly obedient body—her senses would be acute. Accustomed to the exercise of their powers on beautiful objects appropriate to them, they would be truthful in their perceptions, and ready to receive the fullest extent of scientific training. She would speak fluently several languages, write a good hand, sketch with ease and correctness; sing with accuracy; for all these requirements, and many others, would be necessarily obtained by pursuing a complete system of physical development."[2]

In addition, she stressed the importance of fully educating young girls on how their bodies worked. Some of her views were shocking for the time—that girls should be encouraged to engage in all kinds of boisterous play, such as climbing, running, and riding horses, without the burdens of tight, confining clothing; and that marriage should be delayed to prevent or at least postpone the physical strain of childbearing.

The lectures offended some, but inspired others. Later in 1852, she published the lectures as a book called *The Laws of Life with Special Reference to the Physical Education of Girls.*

Perhaps more important, some of the attendees, free-thinking Quaker women, became Blackwell's patients. She delivered their babies and cared for their sick children. Some of their husbands also consulted her. She finally had a practice.

But its growth was too slow for Blackwell's restless ambition. She was treating fairly well-to-do patients, but she was doing nothing to improve the lives of the neediest citizens—the poor, and those with the greatest physical sufferings. Once again, in early 1853, she applied for a post at the New York dispensary and was once again rejected. Having a female physician on staff, she was told, "would not promote the harmonious working of the institution."[3]

THE LITTLE DISPENSARY

In March, Blackwell opened a tiny dispensary near Tompkins Square, in one of the city's worst slum neighborhoods, amid the tenements where poor immigrants lived in unsanitary, crowded conditions. The residents of the buildings shared a common sink, uncollected garbage provided a breeding ground for flies, and nearby slaughterhouses discharged blood into the streets. Pigs roamed the streets at will. Illness was rampant.

On three afternoons every week Blackwell offered medical services to poor patients free of charge. At first, even the poor people were skeptical of a woman doctor. But they had nowhere else to go. She soon had all the patients she could handle. She delivered their babies, treated their illnesses, but perhaps above all, she tried to educate them on the importance of cleanliness, fresh air, a good diet, and exercise. She was becoming a pioneer in the field of public health. The next year, in 1854, she incorporated her little clinic.

In the spring of 1854, Emily graduated "triumphantly,"[4] from Cleveland Medical College. Emily had transferred there after she had experienced problems due to female discrimination in Chicago. The administration of Rush Medical College had had second thoughts about having a female medical student and refused to allow Emily to

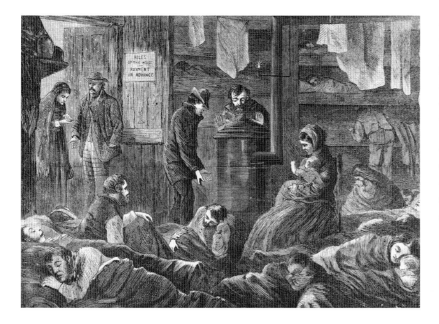

In the mid-1800's, poor immigrants lived in New York City's unsanitary and crowded slums. In March 1853, Blackwell opened a tiny dispensary near Tomkins Square, in one of the city's worst slum neighborhoods, where she offered medical services to poor patients free of charge.

enroll for her second year. Following graduation, Emily went to New York and helped out at the dispensary while she made preparations for clinical study in Europe. She left in the spring, promising to return when she was finished.

In the meantime, Blackwell had to run the dispensary essentially by herself, with limited help from a few male physicians who acted as consultants. But this would soon change, with the arrival of an unexpected visitor later that year.

NEW CONNECTIONS

The unexpected visitor was Marie Zakrzewska, a young woman in her mid-20's. Blackwell learned that Zakrzewska had grown up in Europe. She was the daughter of a midwife, and she had herself received midwife training. Not only that, she had been a professor at a midwifery school in Berlin, Germany. After her sponsor and mentor, the chief of midwifery at the hospital, died, she had come to the United States hoping to study medicine. She wanted to become a doctor. Various obstacles—including lack of money and her inability to speak

English—stood in the way of her getting into a medical school. But then someone had told her about Dr. Elizabeth Blackwell, and she arrived to offer her help at the dispensary.

The two bonded immediately, and Blackwell was overjoyed to have an assistant. She wrote to Emily, "I have at last found a student in whom I can take a great deal of interest. There is true stuff in her, and I shall do my best to bring it out. She must obtain a medical degree."[5] Blackwell set about teaching Zakrzewska English and arranged for her to attend Cleveland Medical College, with the promise that she would return after her graduation. Blackwell was alone again, but now with an end to that loneliness in sight. In a letter to Emily she anticipated the day that she and Zakrzewska would join her. "We may reckon on a little group of three."[6]

In October, Blackwell made an addition to her household. She took in a little girl called Catharine (sometimes spelled Katharine) Barry from the immigration depot on Randall's Island in New York. Blackwell had wanted a servant—"I mean to train [her] up into a valuable domestic, if she prove on sufficient trial to have the qualities, I give her credit for."[7] But after two years in her care, Kitty, as she was usually called, had become something more. Elizabeth recorded in her journal: "On this bright Sunday morning I feel full of hope and strength for the future. Kitty plays beside me with her doll. She has just given me a candy basket, purchased with a penny she had earned, full of delight in 'Doctor's birthday'! Who will ever guess the restorative support which that poor little orphan has been to me?"[8] Kitty stayed with Blackwell the rest of her life.

Blackwell's loneliness was moderating in other ways, too—her family was beginning to gather in New York. In 1853, weary of the disapproval and obstructions placed in her way by her landlady, Blackwell had decided it was time to buy her own home. She found a large one at 79 E. 15th Street. In the fall of 1856, her brother Sam and his new wife, Antoinette Brown, moved in with Blackwell for a few months. Under Blackwell's care, Antoinette soon gave birth to a daughter in the house. Henry and his wife, Lucy Stone, also moved into the big house for a short while, as did Blackwell's mother, Hannah, and her sister Marian. Emily returned from her clinical study in Europe in 1856, and Marie Zakrzewska finished medical school in Cleveland and returned to New York.

A LITTLE GROUP OF THREE

Before her family came to New York, and before her two able medical partners arrived in New York, Blackwell had already started plans for a hospital, which would be for women, staffed entirely by women, and which would provide a place where female medical students could get clinical training.

The opportunities for the latter were still woefully limited; most existing U.S. hospitals still refused to admit women for clinical training. In addition, a physician hostile to the idea of female physicians, Dr. J. Marion Sims, had just opened a women's hospital in the spring of 1855. Blackwell wrote to Emily: "I fear the new Woman's Hospital which they are trying to establish here, will interfere with any plans we may endeavor to carry out—Dr. Sims has never called to see me, and is evidently striving to keep in with the conservatives— . . . all the managers . . . the stiffest of the stiff— . . . all of the fashionable unreformatory set—I think a more unpromising board of managers, as far as any liberal aid to women students goes, could not be selected."[9]

Emily, Marie, and Elizabeth decided to start with a small infirmary with the intention of eventually expanding. As they began to look for backing, however, they were discouraged. Few people believed it could be done. Blackwell recalled the objections they heard: ". . . Female doctors would be looked upon with so much suspicion that the police would interfere; that if deaths occurred their death certificates would not be recognized; that they would be resorted to by classes and persons whom it would be an insult to be called upon to deal with; that without men as resident physicians they would not be able to control the patients . . . and, finally, that they would never be able to collect money enough for so unpopular an effort."[10]

But when had the dire warnings of others ever turned Elizabeth Blackwell from a course she was set on? The three women found a mansion on Bleecker Street.

They immediately geared up fundraising activities in order to raise money for rent, furnishings, and operating costs. Zakrzewska traveled to Boston to get advice from the abolitionist women there, who were old hands at fundraising. She returned with a small donation and the promise to attend a crafts fair to raise money. With the combined efforts of groups in Boston and New York, they were able to raise enough money to get started.

On May 12, 1857, Elizabeth, Marie, and Emily opened the New York Infirmary for Indigent Women and Children. There was a large outpatient clinic and two wards of six beds each, as well as a maternity ward. One floor was set aside for living quarters for the resident physicians, servants, and medical students. Marie would live there, while Emily and Elizabeth would live at Elizabeth's 15th Street home. Elizabeth served as director, Emily as surgeon, and Marie as the resident physician. Though the entire staff was made up of women, a few well-respected male physicians served on the infirmary's consulting board.

"The full thorough education of women in medicine is a new idea. And like all other truths requires time to prove its value."

Elizabeth Blackwell

Prominent progressive New Yorkers attended the opening ceremony, as did the press. The Reverend Henry Ward Beecher, brother of Harriet Beecher Stowe and the Blackwells' old friend from Cincinnati, gave a talk. Her friend William Elder, who had put Blackwell up in Philadelphia at the beginning of her medical journey, also spoke.

Blackwell also said a few words. "The full thorough education of women in medicine is a new idea. And like all other truths requires time to prove its value. Women must show to medical men, even more than to the public, their capacity to act as physicians, their earnestness as students of medicine before the existing institutions with their great advantages of practice and complete organization will be opened to them. They must prove their medical ability before expecting professional recognition."[11]

The infirmary was a success. Most of the patients were Irish and German immigrants from the surrounding neighborhood, and they came in large numbers. In the first seven months, Blackwell and her staff treated over 800 patients. In 1858, the caseload more than doubled. Nurses' training had begun, and five medical students from the women's medical colleges in Philadelphia and Boston also arrived.

Elizabeth, Emily, and Marie ran the little hospital on a weekly budget of only $22 (about $493 today) for food, wages, heat, and lighting. Because most of the patients were treated free of charge—only those who could afford it were charged $4 (about $90 today) a week for inpatient care, barely enough to cover the cost of such services—fundraising was a constant responsibility.

There were a few serious crises in the first two years. One time, a fire broke out in the horse stables located behind the infirmary. Fortunately, the wind blew the flames away from the infirmary and it was spared.

Another time, a riot broke out when a patient died of puerperal fever, an infection that sometimes strikes women after childbirth. A crowd of people waving pickaxes and shovels gathered outside the infirmary, accusing the female doctors of being no better than murderers. Again, the doctors and the infirmary were saved, this time by the appearance of bystanders who quieted the rioters.

But these were isolated incidents in a pattern of high-quality, conscientious care. And, in fact, the women pioneered practices that are standard today. One of these is record-keeping. At the infirmary, the doctors recorded vital information about every patient they treated—name, address, diagnosis, treatment, and outcome. Every prescription was signed by the doctor who wrote it. When male doctors from the established institutions learned of these practices, they were amazed. In addition, basic hygienic rules were always followed. The doctors gave sponges and soap to their patients when they made housecalls and preached cleanliness. They also instructed patients on the need to bathe and keep clean, as well as to ventilate their homes. In this way, the infirmary was truly a modern medical institution.

Chapter 7: Much Work to Do

Elizabeth Blackwell's life blended achievement of her ambitions with a happy personal life: her infirmary was a success, and she was surrounded by her closest family. But she felt deeply that there was much work to do before women would be fully accepted in the medical profession.

Blackwell was focused more on what she needed to accomplish next than what she had already accomplished. And she was frustrated at how little recognition she received for those accomplishments, simply because she was a woman. In an article she wrote for the *Philadelphia Press,* she commented, "When a woman has won herself an honorable position in any unusual line of life, she is still excluded from the companionship and privileges of the class to which she should belong, because her course is unusual."[1]

TRANSATLANTIC TRAVELS

In mid-1857, Blackwell's old friend from England, Barbara Leigh Smith, paid her a visit in New York. She had married a wealthy French doctor and her name was now Barbara Bodichon. Blackwell had long wanted to return to England—she considered it her real home—but there was always too much to do in New York. Now her friend Barbara made the case that she was needed in England, too. In 1858, there were still no female doctors in England. She wanted Blackwell to come to England to lecture about giving women opportunities to enter the medical profession.

There was another reason to go to England—to become the first woman to have her name entered in the British Medical Registry. British physicians had recently set up this registry in order to set uniform standards among physicians in the United Kingdom (U.K.). At that time there were 21 organizations that issued licenses for the practice of medicine in the United Kingdom, and some doctors could practice medicine only in the region under the control of the organization that issued the license. The registry would allow anyone with a license issued by one of these medical organizations to practice anywhere in the United Kingdom. Physicians with non-U.K. degrees would be eligible to register only if they were practicing medicine in the United Kingdom before Oct. 1, 1858. Blackwell had little time to lose if she wanted to open a practice in England before the deadline.

But during this time, a crack, invisible to Blackwell, was opening up in her support system. Emily was becoming increasingly unhappy with her life as a physician. She wrote in her journal on June 20, 1858: "A terrible trial has fallen upon me. An agony of doubt has burnt in my heart for months. Oh my God, is the end of all my aspirations, of my prayers and dreams, to be that this long earnest struggle has been a mistake, that this life of a Physician is so utterly not my life that I can not express myself through it—and worse—worse—that I might have done more in other ways."[2]

"... the Medical Council has registered me as a physician! ...This will be of immeasurable value to the future of medical women in England."

Elizabeth Blackwell, letter to her sister Emily, June 17, 1858

On Aug. 18, 1858, Blackwell, accompanied by Kitty, set sail for London. While in London, she planned to give a series of lectures that would cover general health and disease prevention and promote the idea that women should be allowed to practice medicine. In 1859, with the help of some influential friends from her student days in London, the name Elizabeth Blackwell was entered into the registry. Blackwell wrote to Emily on June 17, "I have only one piece of information to send, but that is of the highest importance—the Medical Council has registered me as a physician! . . .This will be of immeasurable value to the future of medical women in England."[3] It was smaller value, at least in the near term, than Blackwell recognized. Once the council realized that it had registered a woman, it quickly acted to bar women from its rolls in the future.

While in England, Blackwell also visited Florence Nightingale, now famous for her pioneering and heroic work as a battlefield nurse in the Crimean War, fought in what is now Ukraine. But Nightingale had fallen ill during the war and almost died. Now, in January 1859, back in England, though bedridden, Nightingale was working hard to start a school for nurses. She wanted Blackwell to run it.

But Blackwell was not keen on the idea. Her passion was training women to become doctors, not nurses. She noted, besides, a basic incompatibility in their values. In a letter to Bodichon, Blackwell explained it this way: "I could not carry out her plans . . . because it would entirely sacrifice my medical life. . . . She has not realized the importance of opening medicine to women generally—this proceeds partly from her utter faithlessness in medicine—she believes that hygiene and nursing are the only valuable things for sickness, that the physician's action is only injurious, counteracting the useful efforts of nature."[4]

In March, Blackwell delivered a lecture to a packed house at the Marylebone Literary Institution in London. She spoke about her education in the United States and Europe, her founding of the infirmary, her belief in the importance of hygiene in disease prevention. She also touched on the lack of meaningful professional opportunities for educated women. She appealed to women to take up careers in medicine. She said, "The fact that more than half of the ordinary medical practice lies among women and children would seem to be at first sight proof that there is a great deal women could do for themselves. . . . Though they may be few in number, they will be enough to form a new element, another channel by which women in general may draw in and apply to their own needs the active life of the age."[5]

In the audience was a young woman of 22 named Elizabeth Garrett. Like Blackwell, Garrett had been raised by a father who saw no reason to confine his daughters' education to sewing and music. And like Blackwell at her age, Garrett was burning for a career that could give her life meaning.

Blackwell noticed Garrett in the audience. She described seeing her in her autobiography: "The most important listener was the bright, intelligent young lady whose interest in the study of medicine thus aroused."[6] The two would correspond regularly throughout the course of Garrett's medical education and career.

Blackwell delivered lectures in Manchester, Birmingham, and Liverpool, all to enthusiastic response. But plans to start a women's and children's hospital, begun with great enthusiasm, came to nothing when negotiations with a wealthy, but eccentric, French countess named Antonin de Noailles fell through.

BACK TO NEW YORK AND WAR

Now Blackwell had no significant project to keep her in England. In addition, the situation in New York was making her return ever more urgent. In the spring, Marie Zakrzewska had resigned her post at the infirmary to become professor of obstetrics and diseases of women and children at the New England Female Medical College in Boston. That summer, Blackwell went home to New York. In her absence, the trustees of the infirmary had approved a plan to raise $50,000 (about $1,080,000 today) to found a hospital and women's medical college and school of nursing. By the beginning of 1860, the trustees had bought a house at 126 Second Avenue to serve as the new facility. Blackwell and Emily decided to sell the house on 15th Street and moved into the new building.

Blackwell kept busy with her private practice, assisting in the infirmary, and lecturing, while Emily ran the hospital and outpatient clinic and performed all surgery. They had several students, who also served as assistant physicians, and the nursing program had been launched. But Emily could keep her unhappiness a secret no longer. Emily told Blackwell that she intended to quit medicine as soon as she could save up enough money to travel and, perhaps, study art. Blackwell was devastated. She wrote to Barbara Bodichon, "Though I was bitterly disappointed at first, I have now accepted it as inevitable. I used what influence I could at first, but the subject is now never discussed by us—it will at any rate be years before she is in a position to carry out her plans."[7]

All of Emily and Blackwell's plans, along with those of the entire United States, would have to take a back seat to the great calamity that was about to descend on the country. On April 12, 1861, Confederate troops fired on Fort Sumter, in South Carolina, marking the beginning of the American Civil War (1861–1865).

Elizabeth and Emily acted quickly. They called a meeting of the infirmary managers to discuss nursing needs for the war. Someone accidentally placed a notice in the *New York Times,* and a crowd of women, hopeful for an opportunity to help and inspired by the work of the now-famous Florence Nightingale, showed up. A second meeting drew at least 3,000 women.

Out of these meetings developed the Woman's Central Association of Relief. As chair of the registration committee, it was Blackwell's job to screen women who wanted to be war nurses. Even though there was a desperate need for battlefield nurses, the U.S. War Department was reluctant to allow women to serve in that capacity. But even the progess-resistant bureaucrats in Washington, D.C., realized they had no choice. Yes, they agreed, women could serve as nurses, but in order to avoid any impropriety, only the most highly qualified and morally upright women would be accepted as volunteers.

Blackwell delivered lectures on various aspects of nursing to the volunteers. Emily wrote a pamphlet called *The Selection and Training of Nurses*, which was widely used. But neither was permitted any greater involvement in the war effort, despite their desire to do more.

Blackwell wrote to Barbara Bodichon: "We shall do much good, but you will probably not see our names, for we soon found that jealousies were too intense for us to assume our true place. We would have accepted a place on the health commission which our association is endeavoring to establish in Washington, & which the government will probably appoint—but the Doctors would not permit us to come forward. In the hospital committee which you will see referred to in this report, they declined to allow our little hospital to be represented—& they refused to have anything to do with the nurse education plan if 'the Miss Blackwells were going to engineer the matter'—of course as it is essential to open the hospitals to nurses, we kept in the background. Had there been any power to support us, we would have fought for our true place, but there was none—government has declined to recognize women as army nurses. . . As chairman of this Registration Committee we have selected a good amount of excellent material out of the mass that presented itself—and if the Doctors would only do the part they have chosen, & educate that material, we should have a capital band of nurses."[8] This was true. Though Blackwell and Emily were not given any direct involvement in the war, the nurses they helped train were invaluable.

Elizabeth and Emily remained in the New York area throughout the war, running the infirmary. By the time the war ended, the infirmary was treating almost 7,000 patients a year.

In 1866, one of Blackwell's younger brothers, Howard, died suddenly in England. He had been older sister Anna's special favorite, and Elizabeth and Emily read her letters, outpourings of grief, with great concern. Anna had always been the high-strung Blackwell, poetic, idealistic, eccentric, and sensitive. Because of this emotional blow, her younger sisters feared for her mental stability.

Elizabeth traveled to Paris to stay with her grieving sister. While there, Elizabeth visited with Hippolyte Blot. He was married now, with two children.

In 1861, Blackwell became chair of the registration committee of the Woman's Central Association of Relief. Blackwell screened women who wanted to be battlefield nurses during the Civil War.

FOUNDING A MEDICAL SCHOOL

Blackwell returned to New York in the fall of 1866 and got back to work. Throughout the war years and after, Blackwell's chief concern, besides the day-to-day operation of the infirmary, was opening a medical college for women. She promoted the idea in speeches, noting the obstacles women faced in trying to become doctors. She pointed out how many vital resources they were lacking—scholarships, prizes, and other sources of funding; facilities such as libraries, hospitals, and clinics; and professional organizations. She stressed the need for the highest quality education for women so that their qualifications would be comparable to men's. She proposed that her New York Infirmary should serve as the parent institution for a women's medical college.

Bit by bit, plans were made, funds were raised, and a college charter was granted by the state of New York. In November 1868, the Women's Medical College of the New York Infirmary had its first classes, with an enrollment of 15 women. The school's graduation requirements were more rigorous than those at other medical schools. Instead of the customary two years, students were required to complete three years of classwork, and this later would be extended to four years. The school was also a trailblazer in the teaching of hygiene and preventive medicine. Blackwell was professor of hygiene. Emily was professor of obstetrics and diseases of women, with Lucy M. Abbott as her assistant. They also invented a post they called the sanitary visitor. The role of this physician would be to visit the poor and instruct them on hygienic and sanitary practices. She would provide soap and clean towels and sheets and leave informative pamphlets. It was an early form of what is today known as social work.

The relationship between Emily and Elizabeth, however, had begun to grow more strained. Emily was tired of being in her older sister's shadow and under her control. Kitty accidentally overhead a conversation between Marian and Elizabeth, and wrote in her journal, "Aunt Marian told Dr. Elizabeth that she had alienated and was alienating Aunt Emily. My Doctor [Blackwell] wrote to Madame Bodichon about it and Madame Bodichon urged her to come to England and settle there."[9]

Whether that tension played a role in Blackwell's decision to go to Europe is uncertain. But Blackwell knew that Emily was quite adept in running the infirmary. Knowing the infirmary was in capable hands, she could turn her attention to other goals. So in July 1869, Elizabeth left for England. Her goal was to open up medical education for women there.

Before her departure, Elizabeth wrote to Barbara Bodichon: "I am coming with the one strong purpose in my mind of assisting in the establishment, or opening of a thorough medical education for women, in England.—As soon as the Doctorate is freely attainable by English women, I shall feel as if my public work—my own special pioneer mission, were over—but not until then."[10]

She was 48 years old, and she had a new life before her.

Chapter 8: A Pioneer Mission

Elizabeth Blackwell went to England without knowing how long she would stay. She would end up staying there for the remainder of her life—more than 40 years.

During her first months back in England, Blackwell stayed with Barbara Bodichon, but in the spring of 1870 she got her own place in London. She spent the first year or so of her residence in London traveling and making new acquaintances among the prominent citizens of England.

Blackwell began to deliver lectures and work on writing projects. In 1871, she helped form the National Health Society. The purpose of the society, according to an article in *The Times* (London), was to "assist in the formation of local societies, to induce schools to include sanitary instruction in their teachings, to form an office for answering questions, from private individuals and others, as to the proper modes of procedure in cases of sanitary difficulty, and to establish a reference library, with plans, models, and papers."[1] The group came up with the motto *Prevention Is Better Than Cure.*

Blackwell's protégé Elizabeth Garrett, newly married and using the name Elizabeth Garrett Anderson, had successfully become a physician in England, enduring struggles as difficult as Blackwell's many years before. A few years after becoming a doctor, Anderson opened the New Hospital for Women, a 10-bed facility in London, staffed entirely by women. Anderson asked Blackwell to serve as a consulting physician at the hospital, and she agreed, though her position there involved little work and was largely honorary.

In the fall of 1872, Blackwell caught a bad cold that lingered, with chills and fever, for almost two months. To help improve her health, she and Kitty moved out of their house, put their belongings in storage, and embarked on a yearlong journey around Europe.

LONDON SCHOOL OF MEDICINE FOR WOMEN

When she returned to London, Blackwell became active in the new medical school for women that had been established. The mover and shaker behind this project was a woman named Sophia Jex-Blake, who had briefly studied medicine at Elizabeth's infirmary in New York. But Jex-Blake was a problematic character. She was headstrong and lacked tact. These qualities had alienated Elizabeth Garrett Anderson, who otherwise would have been an invaluable ally. Blackwell generally shared this evaluation of Jex-Blake's character, but her response was to involve herself more deeply in the project, in order to provide a more stabilizing influence. She wrote to her brother Sam in 1874: "I find myself at present being drawn in more and more into the organization of a 'London School for Medicine of Women'—a movement was begun here I think rather prematurely by Miss Jex Blake . . . Miss Jex Blake is a dangerous person from her power and want of tact . . . and I now seem compelled to step in and try now for my experience and judgment can supply the control. . . ."[2]

The school opened in October 1874, and Blackwell was an active member of its council. Blackwell remained active with the school in 1875. That year, she was also named lecturer in gynecology. Blackwell held the position for a year, resigning in 1876 because of poor health.

WRITING CAREER

Blackwell, accompanied by Kitty, traveled throughout Europe again beginning in the fall of 1876. Blackwell had begun around this time a book called *Counsel to Parents on the Moral Education of Their Children*. Blackwell knew the book, which she described as "based upon my large medical experience, and observation of the fearful growth of licentiousness in the present generation,"[3] would be highly controversial. But when she sent the book to Emily, she thought it was rather tame, even dull, describing it as "simply a plea for purity of life in both sexes."[4]

Because of its frank discussion of sexual topics, several publishers refused to publish the book, though they admitted to its quality. Blackwell finally found an English publisher, Hatchards, in 1879. The book received positive reviews and turned out to be her most popular work. One review in the British press praised the book: "The solemn and urgent teachings of this little volume should be known to every parent and schoolmaster; and we believe that few young men could peruse it without a quickening of conscience, and a truer sense of the obligations of the moral law."[5]

Around the same time, and after about six years without a permanent home, Blackwell finally found a place that suited her, a small house in Hastings, a village two hours from London by train, overlooking the English Channel. It was called Rock House, and it would be Blackwell's home for the rest of her life.

Blackwell's direct involvement in medicine—either as a teacher or as a physician—had essentially ended by this time. Her moving to Rock House marked the beginning of a period of writing on the topics most important to her—hygiene, religion, sexual ethics, and medical education. Between 1880 and 1898, she published at least one book almost every year. Among her works during this time were *The Human Element in Sex, Scientific Method in Biology,* and *Wrong and Right Methods of Dealing with Social Evil.* In 1895, she published her autobiography, *Pioneer Work in Opening the Medical Profession to Women.*

Blackwell's involvement in social reform causes was extensive during her later years. Besides promoting the ideas spelled out in her books, she also opposed *vivisection*—that is, the use of animals for medical experimentation. This cause became one of her chief interests in the early 1890's.

CHAMPION OF SOCIAL CAUSES

In May 1889, Blackwell renewed her association with the London School of Medicine for Women, becoming a member of the Executive Council. Her address at the opening of the school's winter session that year called on the school to prohibit vivisection.

Blackwell established the Woman's Medical College of the New York Infirmary in 1868. The school trained hundreds of women physicians before it merged with Cornell University Medical School in 1899. This 1870 wood engraving shows an anatomy lecture at the school.

She joined her local branch of the London Anti-Vivisection Society, declaring in a speech in December that "the practice of torturing animals [is] a hindrance to the progress of medical science."[6] She believed that any doctor who could bear to cause animals physical suffering may lack the "intelligent sympathy with suffering"[7] that all genuine healers must possess. She feared that such an attitude toward animals might eventually lead to equally inhumane treatment of poor and powerless human beings in the name of medical progress.

Blackwell also used her influence to speak out against what she considered unnecessary operations performed on women. One of these, the *ovariotomy*, or removal of the ovaries, was a common treatment for various female ailments, including menstrual cramps. One cause that she championed may seem misguided today—she was staunchly opposed to the idea that diseases were caused by germs. But her reasons for objecting to this view—correct as it was—were understandable. She worried that if the understanding of disease was reduced to an invasion of the body by germs, then doctors would stop treating patients holistically—that is, neglect the patient's emotional, spiritual, and environmental situation—and only concern themselves with the disease. The importance of the idea is recognized today in various holistic health approaches.

Blackwell's last years were occupied with pursuit of these causes. As she grew older, however, inevitably she had to deal with the loss of the people close to her. Barbara Bodichon died in 1891. Her sister-in-law Lucy Stone died in 1893. She was devastated at the death of her dog Don in 1896, writing, "The house feels desolate. At dinner I thought how I fed him with juicy bits for his last meal; how he lay by me on the sofa with my arm around him awaiting his unknown fate. This sense of loss makes me ill, I so long for the dear old fellow."[8] She was equally grief-stricken over the death of her other dog, Burr, three years later.

Blackwell cared for her sister Marian after she suffered a stroke. Marian died in August 1897. Anna's death followed in January 1900. Ellen and Sam died in 1901.

In 1906, Blackwell, age 85, and Kitty, about 60, traveled to the United States. It was the only visit she made since moving to England in 1869. She visited with her surviving siblings—Emily, George, and Henry.

In 1907, Blackwell fell down a flight of stairs during a vacation in Scotland. At first it seemed that her injuries were slight, but it soon became apparent that she had suffered some brain damage. Within the next year or two she was unable to leave her house and had lost the ability to speak. In May 1910, Blackwell had a stroke, and died six days later, on May 31. She was 89 years old. According to Blackwell's wishes, Kitty arranged for her body to be buried in Kilmun, Scotland, where they had spent many summer vacations.

Elizabeth Blackwell is remembered for many accomplishments: the first woman doctor; the first woman to be listed on the British Medical Register; a pioneer in the fields of public health, social work, and education; founder of a hospital and medical school for women; and prolific author and lecturer. What drove her was her faith in herself, her keen awareness of social inequities, and her belief that it was not only her duty but her privilege to serve her fellow human beings.

Sixty-eight years earlier, on her graduation from Geneva Medical College, the British humor magazine *Punch* had marked the event with a light-hearted poem. One of the stanzas read:

For Doctrix Blackwell—that's the way
  To dub in rightful gender—
In her profession, ever may
  Prosperity attend her!
Punch, *a gold-handled parasol,*
  Suggests for presentation,
To one so well deserving all
  Esteem and admiration.[9]

Elizabeth had never been blessed with great prosperity; she spent much of her life, including her last few years, in financial straits. She had never been presented with a "gold-handled parasol"—no official organization had ever presented her with an award for her lifetime of service. On the contrary, the sacrifices she made for her causes were many, and her reward could only have been her satisfaction in seeing doors of opportunity open for generations of women who followed her—in medicine and many other professions. ■

Susan La Flesche Picotte (1865–1915)

Only a handful of photos survive showing the first Native American woman physician, Susan La Flesche Picotte. One shows her with two other young women and a child. Susan appears as a slim, pretty teen-ager, thick dark hair parted in the middle and pulled back over her ears. She wears a simple dark dress with a printed scarf. She has a hand affectionately, almost protectively, resting on the back of her sister Marguerite and their friend Mary. Another is a portrait taken when Susan is perhaps in her 30's. The face is now handsome rather than pretty, though her expression shows some strain—fatigue from years of work? sorrow over losses and poor health?—but appears strengthened by determination. A third, taken in 1902, shows Susan with her two sons and her aged mother on the front porch of Susan's home. Susan's frailty is obvious—dark circles under her eyes, thin arms, slightly bent posture. Though her life was not long, it was rich in service to her Omaha people and the effort seems to have marked her.

TRANSITION FROM TRADITION

Susan La Flesche was born on the Omaha Indian reservation in Nebraska on June 17, 1865. She joined a family that already included three older sisters: Susette, 11; Rosalie, 4; and Marguerite, 3; and a half-brother, Francis, who was 8.

Susan's birth coincided with a period of tremendous change for the United States as a whole and especially for American Indians. The 1800's were a time of change and upheaval for all American Indians. As white settlers in search of new land and new opportunities pushed increasingly westward, Indians in the east were forcibly moved from their lands to settle on lands to the west. The result was a domino effect in which Indians from the Great Lakes region, for example, were relocated to lands traditionally occupied by Missouri Valley groups, such as the Osage and Sioux. These groups, in turn, moved westward onto the traditional lands of the Omaha, Oto, and related groups.

At the same time, Indians and whites naturally interacted, sometimes by choice, sometimes by necessity. This created a complex mix of cultural practices, economic alliances, and social interactions. With their mixed white and Indian heritage, both of Susan's parents were products of these interactions.

Susan's father, Joseph La Flesche, Jr., was the son of a French fur trader, Joseph La Flesche, Sr., and an Indian woman named Wa-tun-na. Wa-tun-na's exact ethnic heritage is unclear. Some records and family recollections suggest that she was an Omaha Indian. Others say she was part of a closely related Indian group called the Ponca.

When Joseph, Jr., was a child, his mother left the family and married another man. Joseph, Jr., went to live with relatives among the Dakota Sioux. Later, he went to live with his father. From his teen-age years until his early manhood, Joseph, Jr., traveled with his father on hunting and trading expeditions. During those expeditions, he learned to speak French and various Indian languages, and he had plenty of opportunity to learn white ways. Later, he worked for the American Fur Company and owned a store and a ferry service. Like many people of mixed Indian and European heritage, he straddled the two worlds and tried to forge a compromise between traditional Omaha ways and what he knew would be the ways of the future—the white people's way.

Susan's mother, Mary Gale, was the daughter of a U.S. Army doctor named John Gale and Ni-co-mi, a woman who had mixed Omaha, Oto, and Iowa Indian heritage. John Gale left the family after he was transferred to a new position when Mary was a young girl. He died shortly thereafter. Ni-co-mi married Peter Sarpy, a fur trader of French descent and acquaintance of John Gale. Sarpy sent Mary to be educated in St. Louis, Missouri, where she learned to speak French. Sarpy operated two trading posts. One catered to whites and stood near Council Bluffs, Iowa, on the east side of the Missouri River. The other served Indians and was on the west side of the river near Omaha, Nebraska. Joseph, Jr., became one of Sarpy's employees and possibly a business partner. This connection brought Mary Gale and young Joseph together, and they married in the mid-1840's.

Joseph's leadership qualities must have been evident even as a young man. Big Elk, the Omaha leader who ruled the tribe from the 1810's to the 1840's, took a kind interest in Joseph. Big Elk's son, also called Big Elk, adopted Joseph in the late 1840's or early 1850's. This act made it clear that Joseph was being prepared to take over as chief of the tribe someday. Joseph agreed with the elder Big Elk (and the younger Big Elk) that their people had no choice but to adapt to American ways. The younger Big Elk died shortly after adopting Joseph, and Joseph became one of two principal chiefs of the Omaha Elk clan. After the death of the principal chief of another clan of Omaha, Joseph became the first principal chief of the Omaha tribe. He was called Esta-ma-za, or Iron Eye.

In the 1830's the Omaha began losing control of their traditional lands east of the Missouri River. In 1854, Iron Eye traveled to Washington, D.C., as part of a larger delegation, to sign a treaty that turned over most of the Omaha's traditional homelands in Nebraska to the U.S. government. In return, the Omaha were to receive annual payments from the U.S. government ranging from $10,000 to $40,000 (about $220,000 to $860,000 today), plus other compensation, for the next 30 years. As a result of the treaty, the Omaha were restricted to a 300,000-acre (120,000-hectare) reservation in Nebraska's Blackbird Hills, where Susan would later be born.

Iron Eye was determined to relieve his people of the hardships visited on them by the white people's encroachment and guide them into a new way of life that blended Omaha traditions with white ways. He once said, "After a while the white men came, just as the blackbirds do, and spread over the country . . . it matters not where one looks now one sees white people . . . his only chance is to become as the white man."[1]

Susan La Flesche was born on the Omaha reservation in northeastern Nebraska. She is shown, standing center, *at school in Elizabeth, New Jersey, in 1880, with her friend Mary Tyndall*, left of Susan, *and her older sister Marguerite*, right. *The child at the far left is unidentified.*

Iron Eye was part of a progressive faction within the Omaha tribe called the young men's party. These men were Omaha who did not believe that anything could be gained by resisting the tide of white culture. They had seen their traditional ways overrun by the onslaught of whites. United States government policy discouraged the Omaha from practicing their traditional ways of life, which involved farming part of the year and following the buffalo the rest of the time. United States officials forced the Omaha onto reservations and steered them into taking up full-time farming. No longer could they rely on their annual buffalo hunt for food and clothing because the buffalo were disappearing.

SOMEBODY IN THE WORLD

By the time Susan was born, Iron Eye had built a European-style frame house on the reservation and was successfully farming several acres (or hectares) of crops.

Iron Eye raised Susan and her sisters and brother to survive and succeed by adapting to the white people's ways. He instilled in his children the importance of education and the need to contribute to their society. One day when Susan was about 6, her father said to her and her sisters, "My dear young daughters, do you always want to be simply called those Indians or do you want to go to school and be somebody in the world?"[2]

At the time of Susan's birth in 1865, Iron Eye and those who had joined him in starting farms on the reservation were prospering. His efforts to curb alcohol consumption, increasingly a problem on the reservation, were successful. But Iron Eye was an exception among the Omaha. Others—perhaps less adaptable than Iron Eye or lacking the head start he benefited from as Joseph—suffered from crop failures, disease, and hunger. They also became victims of land-hungry whites. This problem would be a key one for Susan later in her life.

Even though Iron Eye was a devoted and capable ruler, the Omaha agent on the reservation, a U.S. government official, stripped him of his chief's position in 1866. This was a blow to the family's prestige. Who knows whether Susan's life would have been significantly different had Iron Eye kept his leadership of the tribe? But after he lost his position, he seemed to draw the family farther away from traditional Omaha ways. When Susan was a small child, he did not have her take part in the traditional ritual called the Turning of the Child in which she would have received an Omaha name, though her older sister Susette had. As an adult, in her career as an Indian rights activist, Susette was often known by her Indian name, "Bright Eyes."

"My dear young daughters, do you always want to be simply called those Indians or do you want to go to school and be somebody in the world?"

Iron Eye, father of Susan La Flesche Picotte, to his daughters

Susan's first schooling was at a mission school on the reservation run by the Presbyterian church. She started at the age of 3. The Presbyterians saw their purpose as molding young Indians into productive members of white society.

The Presbyterian school closed in 1869, and Susette, now a teen-ager, left to attend the Elizabeth Institute for Young Ladies, in Elizabeth, New Jersey. On the reservation, a school run by the Society of Friends, or Quakers, replaced the Presbyterian school. Susan attended until the age of about 14. At the Quaker school, she studied more rigorous subjects than at the Presbyterian school. According to a letter she wrote to a children's magazine in 1877, Susan studied geography, history, grammar, arithmetic, and spelling. But perhaps most important to her future success, she improved her English skills.

Susette returned home from Elizabeth in 1875. She got a job teaching at the reservation school, and Susan, Rosalie, and Marguerite moved into a small house with her near the school. Neither Susan's father nor mother could or would speak English. But Susette insisted that Susan and her sisters only speak English among themselves.

A CALLING AND A GIFT FOR MEDICINE

When Susan was young, she once visited an Omaha woman on the reservation who was very ill. That night, as the woman's condition worsened, the white doctor, employed by the government to care for the residents of the reservation, was called. In spite of repeated requests for his attention, he never came. Later when Susan recalled this event, her anger showed. That doctor, she said, would rather hunt prairie chickens than care for "poor, suffering humanity."[3] She said later that this experience gave her the willpower to study medicine.

Picotte's oldest sister, Susette, was a well-known Indian rights activist. She is shown in a photo from about 1890.

Sometime around 1879, Susan's sister Susette began to attract notice as an Indian rights activist, touring the East and delivering lectures on the forced removal of the Ponca Indians from their Nebraska homeland. Susette's fame and influence helped Susan and Marguerite get accepted to the Elizabeth Institute, and Susan studied there for more than two years. Few records remain of her years at Elizabeth, so little is known about her experiences there. What is known is that the curriculum included English, Latin, French, German, philosophy, and physiology, so she must have studied at least some of these subjects.

In 1882, at the age of 17, Susan returned to the reservation. She spent the next two years working at the Quaker mission school and taught a class of young children.

In 1882, legislation passed in U.S. Congress to allow the Omaha people to divide their land for private ownership. An *anthropologist* (a scientist who studies humanity and human culture) named Alice Fletcher came to the reservation to help the Omaha divide their land. Susan's half-brother, Francis, had become friends with Fletcher when he met her while working as an interpreter for a lecture tour in the Midwest and East in 1879. In 1881, Fletcher visited the reservation to study Omaha culture. In the summer of 1883, Fletcher became so ill that she was confined to bed for several weeks. During her convalescence, Susan helped to care for her. This experience must have given Susan some taste of what medical work might be like. Perhaps it showed her that she had a gift for it. It may have been during her long hours with Fletcher that Susan first talked to her friend about becoming a doctor, so that she could teach the Omaha people how to stay healthy and care for them when they were sick.

In 1884, La Flesche left the reservation once again, this time to attend the Hampton Normal and Agricultural Institute, in Hampton, Virginia. The institute had been founded in 1868 to educate freed, black slaves and it opened its doors to Indian students in 1878. She started classes there in August 1884, taking up residence in a girls' dormitory in a comfortable room. She was happy and thrived at the school, both academically and socially. She was also active in a wide variety of volunteer work. She belonged to a group called the Lend-a-Hand Club, which acted on behalf of the poor, and also volunteered in the cause of *temperance* (the principle and practice of not using alcoholic drink). Another group Susan belonged to, called the Christian Endeavor Society, taught religious doctrine.

At Hampton, her studies were made pleasant by a variety of recreational activities and friendships with fellow students. She developed a close and loving friendship with a young Sioux man named Thomas Ikinicapi. His background was not as cultured as hers and, unlike the academically gifted Susan, he struggled with his studies. His health was also delicate. Although some people discouraged her from the relationship, she was undeterred. She continued to see him, and described him as *"without exception* the handsomest Indian I ever saw."[4]

At Hampton Susan also got to know the school physician, Martha M. Waldron. Waldron encouraged Susan to consider medicine as a career. Waldron cared deeply about the health problems of Indians on reservations, and she probably saw in Susan a perfect candidate to fill the role of healer and educator.

Letters that survive from the time clearly show Susan's attitudes toward the Indians' place in American society. She believed, like her father, that success for Indians depended on Indians becoming "civilized," which translated into learning and adopting white ways. To Susan, those who did not share such beliefs were "nonprogressives." So to her, making progress for Indians was synonymous with becoming white. But this is not to say that she wanted to deny her Omaha heritage. In fact, she was proud of it.

On May 20, 1886, Susan graduated from the Hampton Institute as *salutatorian* (the student who delivers the address of welcome at the graduation of a class; usually second highest in the class). Her speech, "My Childhood and Womanhood," recalled the happy details of her childhood in Nebraska. But she expressed her conviction, absorbed from her father, that the future of her people depended on their learning to adapt to a changing world. She said, "We have to prepare our people to live in the white man's way, to use the white man's books, and to use his laws. . . ."[5] She also expressed

> *"We have to prepare our people to live in the white man's way, to use the white man's books, and to use his laws. . . ."*
>
> Susan La Flesche Picotte, "My Childhood and Womanhood," *Southern Workman,* July 1886

appreciation for the educational system that she benefited from and asked those in the audience in the position to do so, to "help us climb higher."[6] She also outlined her personal goals and what she wanted to accomplish as a physician. She wanted to teach the Omaha "the importance of cleanliness, order, and ventilation, how to take care of their bodies as well as care for their souls."[7]

Her educational experience at Hampton was a success. Not only was she salutatorian, but she also won the Demorest Prize for academic achievement.

During her two years at Hampton, Susan studied literature, geography, math, physiology, English, government, history, politics, and biology. She also taught during the summer. This curriculum was designed primarily to give Hampton students a vocational education. But Susan had another career goal. Even before her graduation, she had already started the process of applying to the Woman's Medical College of Pennsylvania, in Philadelphia.

FIRST NATIVE AMERICAN WOMAN PHYSICIAN

One of the first orders of business in applying to the college was obtaining a letter of recommendation. But the most difficult challenge was not getting accepted to medical school, it was amassing the money needed for tuition and other expenses.

In 1886, Waldron wrote to the Woman's Medical College of Pennsylvania to recommend Susan for a scholarship. But her request was turned down. Alice Fletcher did all she could to help Susan. Fletcher worked her contacts to get funding for Susan's medical education. She put Susan's case to Sara Thomson Kinney, who was president of the Connecticut Indian Association. The association was a group of wealthy white women who dedicated themselves to Indian causes. Kinney approached the commissioner at the Office of Indian Affairs, an agency within the U.S. Department of the Interior that dealt with trade, negotiations, and other matters involving Indians, for help in sponsoring Susan's education. Susan was accepted by the Woman's Medical College during the summer. The Connecticut Indian Association agreed to pay for all of Susan's education, and the Office of Indian Affairs provided an additional stipend. After some delays, Susan's funding came through shortly after she had arrived at the college to start her medical training.

MEDICAL STUDENT

In a letter she wrote home after she began her studies, Susan told of her fascination with *anatomy* (the study of the biological structure of living things). She said that dissecting cadavers did not bother her all. In fact, she quite matter-of-factly described the dissection routine: "Six students take one body. . . Two take the head . . . two the chest . . . two the abdomen and legs. Then we take off little by little."[8] She also studied chemistry, *physiology* (the study of how living things function), *histology* (the biological science that studies the structure of the tissues of organisms), general therapeutics, and *obstetrics* (the branch of medicine and surgery concerned with treating women before, in, and after childbirth), and observed surgeries.

Her sister Marguerite was still at Hampton, and for Christmas break 1886 Susan traveled there. During this visit, she was also reunited with Thomas Ikinicapi. Although they both were clearly very fond of each other, Susan did not let the relationship develop further. She had promised her sponsors that she would not marry until she had completed her education.

During 1887, Susan continued her studies, passed her exams, and continued her volunteer work. She became secretary of the Young Women's Christian Association (YWCA) and continued her work with the Christian Endeavor Society. She visited Indian orphans at Philadelphia facilities.

Philadelphia was a cultural education for Susan La Flesche as well. She attended concerts, the opera, and museums, and toured historical sites. She also made contacts among the influential people of Philadelphia. These friends would later become a valuable source of aid when she needed material help for her work as physician on the Omaha reservation.

After passing her exams in the spring of 1888, she finally had the opportunity to make a visit home, for the first time in two years. While there, she helped to care for her ailing parents. In September 1888, her father, Iron Eye, died.

The following March, Susan La Flesche graduated. When she was handed her diploma, she officially became the first Native American woman physician. Shortly afterward, she competed for, and won, an internship at the Woman's Hospital, in Philadelphia.

After her graduation, the first woman Native American doctor embarked on a lecture tour of Connecticut sponsored by her benefactors at the Connecticut Indian Association (CIA). The purpose of the tour was to gain support for the CIA. In that respect, it was a great success, and CIA membership increased significantly.

La Flesche received important clinical experience during her internship in Philadelphia. She also made the rounds of poor neighborhoods, caring for the people there. In August 1889, she accepted a position as the doctor for the boarding school at the Omaha Agency in Nebraska. She set out for home.

RESERVATION PHYSICIAN ADVOCATE

La Flesche's government job was as a physician, but she incorporated many teaching responsibilities in her activities, instructing the students in hygiene and basic nursing skills. She set up an office at the school, where she saw patients from all over the reservation. Her services were immediately in demand. The people, who had become used to spotty care from white male doctors assigned to them by the Office of Indian Affairs, appreciated having a doctor who was one of their own people and spoke their language.

Still, some Omaha did not trust white medicine, even if it was practiced by an Omaha. They preferred their traditional ways of healing. But La Flesche won over some of the skeptics by curing a sick young boy. She prescribed a treatment and by the next day he had recovered. Word spread throughout the reservation. After La Flesche had been back on the reservation only a few months, most of the Indians had switched from the reservation doctor to her. Soon she was so busy treating patients that she cut back on some of her responsibilities at the boarding school, and the government officially appointed her physician for the entire reservation.

Much of her medical work required La Flesche to make house calls in all weather throughout the widespread reservation. At first she rode on horseback. But the jolting and bouncing broke her bottles of medicine and thermometers. Eventually she was able to buy a carriage and a team of horses. She treated a wide range of contagious diseases, including flu, dysentery, cholera, and an eye disease called conjunctivitis. She worked hard not only to heal the people but to teach them basic preventive methods, such as isolation of sick people and avoiding sharing towels and basins with the sick. Her care prevented many deaths from the flu. But medical science at the time had not yet developed treatments for more serious diseases, such as tuberculosis, and there was little she could do. In the 1890's, tuberculosis took many lives on the reservation.

Another disease, one that in many ways was more complicated to treat, occupied more and more of Susan's time in the 1890's. This disease was alcoholism.

Picotte worked to improve medical care on the Omaha reservation. From about 1891 to 1894, she was head physician on the reservation. She is shown second from left at a peyote religious meeting on the reservation.

Though alcoholism was not defined as a disease as such in the 1800's, the dangers and ill effects of heavy alcohol use were well known. La Flesche's father had worked to curb alcohol abuse among the Omaha years earlier, instituting policies to punish drunkenness. Alcoholism had become a major social problem among the Indians in the early years of the 1800's, as fur traders introduced whiskey and other strong alcoholic beverages to the Indians. Now, La Flesche was faced with an increasing alcohol problem among her people.

La Flesche worked to pass laws that would prohibit the sale of alcohol in towns established on the reservation and close down saloons in surrounding towns. She also wrote letters asking for funding to support temperance efforts, to start a reservation police force, and to pass antialcohol laws. She continued to work for prohibition throughout the 1890's and into the 1900's. But her efforts were only partly successful, and alcoholism continued to take its toll on her people.

Because of La Flesche's mainstream education and English skills, it was not long before many Omaha turned to her for translation and letter-writing services, as well. In 1887, the Omaha had been granted U.S. citizenship, and the Dawes Act had granted them the right to own land individually on the reservation. Helping her fellow Omaha sort out the legal and financial issues involved in these land transfers would eventually become a big part of her work on the reservation. La Flesche gave much time to helping the Omaha arrange land transfers and obtain payments due them. She worked to protect the Omaha as best she could from unscrupulous land dealers, some of whom used such tactics as giving the Indians alcohol and having them sign away their land when they were drunk.

These land policies had another bad effect. They made a long-standing problem among the Omaha—alcoholism—even worse. Omaha Indians who had sold their land sometimes found themselves with a lot of money but nothing to do. Some, adrift in idleness, spent their money on alcohol. Others squandered it foolishly on friends and family and found themselves in hopeless poverty. The problem was often made worse by whites who made money selling alcohol to the Indians.

PRIVATE LIFE, PUBLIC ROLE

La Flesche had difficulties of her own during the 1890's. Her health, always somewhat delicate, had begun to fail. In December 1892, she came down with an illness that caused her severe pain in the head, neck, and ears. This illness kept her in bed for several weeks. In the spring, she had an accident in her carriage and her injuries prevented her from working for a time. The following fall, she got sick again and could not work for several weeks. Then her mother became ill and needed care. In order to care for her mother, Susan resigned her position as reservation doctor in November 1893.

In 1892, the husband of La Flesche's sister Marguerite, Charles Picotte, died. His brother Henry (a farmer of French and Sioux Indian ancestry) arrived on the reservation. Susan and Henry fell in love and married in 1894.

The couple moved to Bancroft, Nebraska, where Susan La Flesche Picotte started a private medical practice. Her patients included both whites and Indians. But her health continued to be an obstacle. In the summer of 1897, Susan's mysterious recurring illness struck again. This time she became so ill that her family and friends feared for her life. But she once again recovered. Susan and Henry had two sons, Caryl and Pierre.

For the next eight years, Susan and Henry raised their two sons. Picotte served her people as a doctor while also performing charity work and promoting temperance and Christianity with her writing and lecturing. But personal tragedy struck in 1905. Henry, who had long been a heavy drinker and who had also suffered from tuberculosis, died. Picotte was heartbroken. She wrote to a friend that at times she so longed for him that she could "almost go wild."[9]

"We have rules and regulations to the right of us, . . . to the left of us, . . . behind us; do you wonder we object to continuation of them in front of us?"

Susan La Flesche Picotte to *Omaha Bee,* 1909

After her husband died, the local Presbyterian church hired Picotte as its missionary to the Omaha people, the first Indian ever to serve in such a position. She moved her family to a two-story house in Walthill, Nebraska, that she had built, according to her specifications, with many windows as well as a furnace and an indoor bathroom. During Sunday services Picotte read the bible in the Omaha language and interpreted hymns. Though few Omaha attended at first, before long, her services were drawing dozens of people. She also taught in Sunday school, and she credited the spreading of the message of salvation with the reduction in heavy drinking on the reservation. In a report to the church, she wrote, "The women are drinking much less, and are taking care of their homes and of their children."[10]

In the meantime, Picotte also took on the frustrating and seemingly endless job of advocating on behalf of the Omaha with the U.S. government. In the late 1800's and early 1900's, Indians had to wend their way through a bewildering array of regulations and laws, many of which restricted their ability to make their own financial decisions. In 1909, Susan wrote, "We have rules and regulations to the right of us, . . . to the left of us, . . . behind us; do you wonder we object to continuation of them in front of us?"[11]

Many of these regulations had to do with land and money. For example, the Omaha had to ask the Omaha Indian agent, who represented the U.S. government on the reservation, for permission to spend money set aside in trusts for them—from small expenditures, as for food or a blanket, to more significant ones, as for surgical procedures. This process involved filling out extensive paperwork. Often approval was months in coming. Susan wrote of a number of cases in which sick Omaha died while waiting for the release of money to pay for medical treatment. In some cases, the money arrived long after the individuals died, thus denying them even a decent funeral.

These regulations were based on the government's belief that most of the Indians were too unsophisticated to make their own financial decisions. Some of the most troublesome were regulations having to do with land ownership. Since 1882, the Omaha Allotment Act assigned plots of reservation land to individuals. This act was supposed to encourage the Omaha to become independent farmers, just like the white settlers. Though the Omaha technically owned their land, they were not allowed to sell or lease it.

These regulations were a double-edged sword. In some ways they protected the Indians from unscrupulous white land dealers who employed all kinds of tricks to separate the Indians from their land. But at the same time, they were extremely insulting to the Omaha people, who were fairly well-educated compared with most Indians and even whites in the region. Picotte understood the dilemma. If the Indians were granted more freedom to sell or lease their land, they potentially would be open to more abuse by opportunistic land dealers.

In spite of her misgivings, however, Picotte threw her influence on the side of increased rights for her people. In 1910, although in continued poor health, she agreed to travel to Washington, D.C., with a delegation, to lobby on behalf of the lifting of the land regulations. She addressed the U.S. Secretary of the Interior and asked that the Omaha be given the same property rights as white citizens. The request was ultimately granted. The result of this hard-earned freedom was that by 1910, few Omaha were farming their own land. Instead, most of them earned a living through land sales and land rental income and by working as unskilled laborers for whites. The vast majority either sold their land outright or mortgaged the land and, with no other source of income, had no hope of repaying the mortgage. Picotte blamed the plight of the Indians on the government. Living for so long under the regulations that prohibited them from making their own financial decisions had deprived them of the opportunity to learn how to manage their money and property in the dominant white culture. "If we are incompetent today, it is because we have been kept from developing as we ought to have by experiences gained through . . . contact with the white man,"[12] Picotte said.

Picotte may or may not have realized it, but in 1910, at the age of only 45, she was already nearing the end of her life. The constant illnesses—centered, it seemed, on the bones of her face—had never fully cleared up. She had had a full and busy life, filled with accomplishments, victories, sadness, and mostly much hard work on behalf of her people. She had accomplished many of the things she set out to do.

Picotte, left, *is shown in 1902 with her mother, Mary Gale, and her sons, Caryl and Pierre, at home in Bancroft, Nebraska, where she practiced medicine and her husband Henry Picotte farmed.*

But one long-held dream still eluded Picotte—a hospital for the Omaha people. Over the years, she had tried many times to raise money to build a hospital, but she was never successful. By 1911, the reservation had many towns. The transportation system included roads and railway lines. Picotte now had the support of a community of whites and Indians alike. Together, they raised $8,500 (about $167,000 today) and the land needed. And in January 1913, the hospital, on a hilltop in Walthill, opened.

In 1915, Picotte had two operations on her facial bones. The operations failed, and on Sept. 18, 1915, Picotte died.

A photo shows a large granite headstone in an almost treeless Nebraska cemetery, with the name Picotte in bold block letters emblazoned across the top. It is the gravesite of Susan La Flesche Picotte and her husband, Henry. Susan was laid to rest at the relatively young age of 50, after serving her people tirelessly and selflessly as a physician, teacher, activist, and community leader. ■

Notes

ELIZABETH GARRETT ANDERSON

1. *The Lancet*, 18 June 1870; qtd. in Jo Manton, *Elizabeth Garrett Anderson* (New York: Dutton, 1965) 192.
2. Elizabeth Garrett, MS draft for a speech, Royal Free Hospital School of Medicine; qtd. in Manton 44.
3. Qtd. in Manton 51.
4. Elizabeth Garrett to Emily Davies, 15 June 1860, Fawcett Library; reprinted in Louisa Garrett Anderson, *Elizabeth Garrett Anderson, 1836–1917* (London: Faber and Faber Limited, 1939) 46.
5. Newson Garrett to Elizabeth Garrett, 8 July 1860; reprinted in Louisa Garrett Anderson 56.
6. Qtd. in Manton 109.
7. Qtd. in Louisa Garrett Anderson 125.
8. *British Medical Journal*, 18 June 1870; qtd. in Manton 192.
9. Elizabeth Garrett, MS draft for a speech, Royal Free Hospital School of Medicine; qtd. in Manton 230.
10. Qtd. in Manton 346.

ELIZABETH BLACKWELL

Introduction
1. Elizabeth Blackwell, Diary, 1 Aug. 1902 (Blackwell Family Papers, Library of Congress); qtd. in Nancy Ann Sahli. *Elizabeth Blackwell, M.D. (1821–1910): A New Biography.* (New York: Arno Press, 1982) 439.

Chapter 1
1. Elizabeth Blackwell, *Pioneer Work in Opening the Medical Profession to Women* (1895; New York: Schocken Books, 1977) 3.
2. Anna Blackwell Memoirs, typed copy (Blackwell Family Papers, Schlesinger Library, Radcliffe College), 90; qtd. in Sahli 9.

Chapter 2
1. Elizabeth Blackwell, Diary, 10 May 1836 (Blackwell Family Papers, Library of Congress); qtd. in Sahli 14.
2. Elizabeth Blackwell, Diary, 14 March 1838 (Blackwell Family Papers, Library of Congress); qtd. in Sahli 17.
3. Elizabeth Blackwell, Diary, 2 March 1838 (Blackwell Family Papers, Library of Congress); qtd. in Sahli 19.
4. Elizabeth Blackwell, Diary, 12 May 1838 (Blackwell Family Papers, Library of Congress); qtd. in Sahli 21.
5. Elizabeth Blackwell, Diary, 6-8 Aug. 1838 (Blackwell Family Papers, Library of Congress); qtd. in Sahli 22.
6. Elizabeth Blackwell, Diary, 12 Nov. 1838 (Blackwell Family Papers, Library of Congress); qtd. in Sahli 23.
7. Blackwell, *Pioneer Work* 13.
8. Blackwell, *Pioneer Work* 15.
9. Blackwell, *Pioneer Work* 16.
10. Blackwell, *Pioneer Work* 22.
11. Blackwell, *Pioneer Work* 21.
12. Blackwell, *Pioneer Work* 24.
13. Blackwell, *Pioneer Work* 23.
14. Blackwell, *Pioneer Work* 24-25.
15. Blackwell, *Pioneer Work* 24-25.

Chapter 3
1. Blackwell, *Pioneer Work* 27.
2. Elizabeth Blackwell, MS autobiography (Blackwell Family Papers, Schlesinger Library, Radcliffe College); qtd. in Sahli 48-49.
3. John Ware, *Remarks on the Employment of Females as Practitioners in Midwifery, By a Physician* (Boston, 1820), 7; qtd. in Morantz-Sanchez, Regina, *Sympathy and Science: Women Physicians in American Medicine.* 2nd ed. (Chapel Hill, N.C.: University of North Carolina Press, 2000) 27.
4. Ware 27.
5. Blackwell, *Pioneer Work* 31.
6. Blackwell, *Pioneer Work* 31.
7. Blackwell, *Pioneer Work* 34.

8. Blackwell, *Pioneer Work* 34-35.

9. Blackwell, *Pioneer Work* 41.

Chapter 4

1. Elizabeth Blackwell to Hannah Blackwell, 27 July 1845 (Blackwell Family Papers, Library of Congress); qtd. in Sahli 55.

2. Elizabeth Blackwell to Marian Blackwell, July 7, 1846, (Blackwell Family Papers, Library of Congress); qtd. in Sahli 57.

3. Blackwell, *Pioneer Work* 59.

4. Blackwell, *Pioneer Work* 61.

5. Quoted in Nancy Kline, *Elizabeth Blackwell: A Doctor's Triumph* (Berkeley, Cal.: Conari Press, 1997) 72.

6. Blackwell, *Pioneer Work* 65-66.

7. Blackwell, *Pioneer Work* 70.

8. Blackwell, *Pioneer Work* 67.

9. Blackwell, *Pioneer Work* 68.

10. Blackwell, *Pioneer Work* 79.

11. Qtd. in Kline 92.

12. Elizabeth Blackwell, *Buffalo Medical Journal and Monthly Review*, IV, No. 9, 531; qtd. in Sahli 77.

13. Blackwell, *Pioneer Work* 81.

14. Blackwell, *Pioneer Work* 83-84.

15. Blackwell, *Pioneer Work* 85.

16. Blackwell, *Pioneer Work* 89-90.

17. Blackwell, *Pioneer Work* 87.

18. *Geneva Gazette*, 26 Jan. 1849; qtd. in Sahli 75.

Chapter 5

1. Blackwell, *Pioneer Work* 109.

2. Blackwell, *Pioneer Work* 127.

3. Blackwell, *Pioneer Work* 127.

4. Blackwell, *Pioneer Work* 143.

5. Anna Blackwell to Blackwell Family, 22 Nov. 1849 (Blackwell Family Papers, Library of Congress); qtd. in Sahli 82.

6. Qtd. in Elinor Rice Hays, *Those Extraordinary Blackwells* (New York: Harcourt, Brace & World, 1967) 87.

7. Blackwell, *Pioneer Work* 156.

8. Elizabeth Blackwell to Emily Blackwell, 5 June 1850; qtd. in Hays 87.

9. Blackwell, *Pioneer Work* 157.

10. Samuel C. Blackwell, Journal, 3 Feb. 1850 (Blackwell Family Papers, Schlesinger Library, Radcliffe College); qtd. in Sahli 83.

11. Elizabeth Blackwell, Gräfenberg Diary, 24 June 1850 (Blackwell Family Papers, Library of Congress); qtd. in Sahli 85-86.

12. Qtd. in Ishbel Ross, *Child of Destiny: The Life Story of the First Woman Doctor* (New York: Harper & Brothers, 1949) 155.

13. Blackwell, *Pioneer Work* 171.

14. Elizabeth Blackwell to Lady Noel Byron, 29 Mar. 1851 (Blackwell Family Papers, Library of Congress); qtd. in Sahli 90.

15. Blackwell, *Pioneer Work* 180.

Chapter 6

1. *New York Daily Times*, 1 Mar. 1852; qtd. in Sahli 119.

2. Elizabeth Blackwell, *The Laws of Life with Special Reference to the Physical Education of Girls.* (New York, George P. Putnam, 1852); qtd. in Sahli 122.

3. Qtd. in E. Moberly Bell, *Storming the Citadel: The Rise of the Woman Doctor* (London: Constable & Company Ltd, 1953) 41.

4. Dr. Nancy Clark, qtd. in Dorothy Clarke Wilson, *Lone Woman: The Story of Elizabeth Blackwell, The First Woman Doctor* (Boston: Little, Brown and Company, 1970), 309.

5. Qtd. in Kline 142.

6. Blackwell, *Pioneer Work* 205.

7. Elizabeth Blackwell to Emily Blackwell, 1 Oct. 1856 (Blackwell Family Papers, Library of Congress); qtd. in Sahli 128.

8. Blackwell, *Pioneer Work* 198.

9. Elizabeth Blackwell to Emily Blackwell, undated (Blackwell Family Papers, Library of Congress); qtd. in Sahli 130.

10. Qtd. in Kline 149.

11. Qtd. in Ross 203-204.

Chapter 7

1. Elizabeth Blackwell, "The Position of Women," *The Philadelphia Press*, 25 Aug. 1857; qtd. in Sahli 136.

2. Emily Blackwell, Diary, 20 June 1858 (Blackwell Family Papers, Schlesinger Library, Radcliffe College); qtd. in Kline 156.

3. Blackwell, *Pioneer Work* 226.

4. Elizabeth Blackwell to Barbara Bodichon, 29 Jan. 1859 (Elizabeth Blackwell Collection, Special Collections, Columbia University Library): qtd. in Sahli 139.

5. Qtd. in Jo Manton, *Elizabeth Garrett Anderson* (New York: Dutton, 1965) 51.

6. Blackwell, *Pioneer Work* 218.

7. Elizabeth Blackwell to Barbara Bodichon, 2 Dec. 1860 (Elizabeth Blackwell Collection, Special Collections, Columbia University Library): qtd. in Sahli 148.

8. Elizabeth Blackwell to Barbara Bodichon, 5 June 1861 (Elizabeth Blackwell Collection, Special Collections, Columbia University Library): qtd. in Sahli 150-151.

9. Kitty Barry Blackwell, Reminiscences (Blackwell Family Papers, Library of Congress), 41 A-42; qtd. in Sahli 167-168.

10. Elizabeth Blackwell to Barbara Bodichon, June 16, 1869 (Elizabeth Blackwell Collection, Special Collections, Columbia University Library): qtd. in Sahli 168.

Chapter 8

1. *The Times* (London), 13 May 1872; qtd. in Sahli 205-206.

2. Elizabeth Blackwell to Samuel C. Blackwell, 21 Sept. 1874 (Blackwell Family Papers, Library of Congress); qtd. in Sahli 217.

3. Elizabeth Blackwell to Samuel C. Blackwell, 2 June 1877 (Blackwell Family Papers, Library of Congress); qtd. in Sahli 230.

4. Emily Blackwell to Lucy Stone, 29 Jan. 1879 (Blackwell Family Papers, Library of Congress); qtd. in Sahli 235.

5. Qtd. in Sahli 267.

6. *Hastings and St. Leonards Observer*, 14 Dec. 1889; qtd. in Sahli 352.

7. Qtd. in Kline 175.

8. Elizabeth Blackwell, MS description of Don's burial, on cash account page in

Diary, 1896 (Blackwell Family Papers, Library of Congress); qtd. in Sahli 426-427.

9. *Punch* 1849; qtd. in Blackwell, *Pioneer Work* 261.

SUSAN LA FLESCHE PICOTTE

1. Senate Misc. Doc. No. 31, 47th Cong., 1st sess.; qtd. in Alice C. Fletcher and Francis La Flesche, *The Omaha Tribe*, Bureau of American Ethnology Twenty-Seventh Annual Report, 1905-1906, Washington, D.C.: Government Printing Office, 1911, 73-74, Reprint, 2 vols., Lincoln, Neb.: University of Nebraska Press, 1972, 638.

2. Dr. Susan Picot, Indian Physician Dead at Walthill," *Walthill Times,* 18 Sept. 1915; qtd. in Benson Tong, *Susan La Flesche Picotte, M.D.: Omaha Indian Leader and Reformer* (Norman, Okla.: University of Oklahoma Press, 1999) 55.

3. Susan La Flesche to J. M. Gould, 2 Sept. 1887; reprinted in "The Indian," scrapbook, 1 (Sara Thomson Kinney Papers, Connecticut State Library, Hartford, Connecticut); qtd. in Tong 56.

4. Susan La Flesche to Rosalie La Flesche Farley, 24 Oct. 1886, Nebraska State Historical Society, Lincoln, Nebraska; qtd. in Peggy Pascoe, *Relations of Rescue: The Search for Female Moral Authority in the American West, 1874-1939* (Oxford: Oxford University Press, 1990; Reprint, New York: Oxford University Press, 1991) 152.

5. Susan La Flesche, "My Childhood and Womanhood," *Southern Workman,* July 1886, 78; qtd. in Pascoe 124.

6. Susan La Flesche, "My Childhood and Womanhood," *Southern Workman,* July 1886, 78; qtd. in Tong 64.

7. Susan La Flesche, "My Childhood and Womanhood," *Southern Workman,* July 1886, qtd. in Tong 64.

8. Susan La Flesche to Rosalie La Flesche Farley, 17 Nov. 1886, La Flesche Family Papers, Nebraska State Historical Society, Lincoln, Nebraska; qtd. in Tong 73.

9. Susan La Flesche to My dear friend,

12 Oct. 1905, Susan La Flesche Alumni File, Hampton University Archives, Hampton, Virginia; qtd. in Tong 122.

10. Susan La Flesche, "The Varied Work of an Indian Missionary," *Home Mission Monthly* 22 (August 1908), 247; qtd. in Tong 125.

11. Susan La Flesche to *Omaha Bee*, 1909; qtd. in Norma Kidd Green, *Iron Eye's Family: The Children of Joseph La Flesche* (Lincoln, Neb.: Johnsen Publishing Company, 1969) 156.

12. Qtd. in Tong 159-160.

Recommended Reading

BOOKS

Blackwell, Elizabeth. *Pioneer Work in Opening the Medical Profession to Women.* New York: Longmans, Green, 1895.

Brown, Marion Marsh. *Homeward the Arrow's Flight.* Nashville: Abingdon, 1980.

Chambers, Peggy. *A Doctor Alone: A Biography of Elizabeth Blackwell.* New York: Abelard-Schuman, 1958.

Fancourt, Mary St. J. *They Dared to be Doctors: Elizabeth Blackwell [and] Elizabeth Garrett Anderson.* London: Longmans, Green, 1965.

Hays, Elinor Rice. *Those Extraordinary Blackwells: The Story of a Journey to a Better World.* New York: Harcourt, 1967.

Kline, Nancy. *Elizabeth Blackwell: A Doctor's Triumph.* Berkeley: Conari, 1997.

Manton, Jo. *Elizabeth Garrett Anderson.* New York: Dutton, 1965.

Morantz-Sanchez, Regina Markell. *Sympathy and Science: Women Physicians in American Medicine.* New York: Oxford, 1985.

Ross, Ishbel. *Child of Destiny: The Life Story of the First Woman Doctor.* New York: Harper, 1949.

Sahli, Nancy Ann. *Elizabeth Blackwell, M.D. (1821–1910): A Biography.* 1974. New York: Arno, 1982.

Tong, Benson. *Susan La Flesche Picotte, M.D.: Omaha Indian Leader and Reformer.* Norman: Univ. of Okla. Pr., 1999.

Windsor, Laura Lynn. *Women in Medicine: An Encyclopedia.* Santa Barbara: ABC-CLIO, 2002.

WEB SITES

"Changing the Face of Medicine: Dr. Susan La Flesche Picotte." *National Library of Medicine.* National Institutes of Health, Department of Health & Human Services. <http://www.nlm.nih.gov/changingthefaceofmedicine/physicians/biography_253.html>

"Elizabeth Blackwell, M.D." *Hobart and William Smith Colleges.* <http://campus.hws.edu/his/blackwell/>

"Elizabeth Blackwell – That girl there is doctor of medicine." *National Library of Medicine.* National Institutes of Health, Department of Health & Human Services. Online version of an exhibit held at the National Library of Medicine, Jan. 23–Sept. 4., 1999. <http://www.nlm.nih.gov/hmd/blackwell/>

"Historic Figures: Elizabeth Garrett Anderson (1836–1917)." *BBC.co.uk.* The British Broadcasting Corporation. <http://www.bbc.co.uk/history/historic_figures/garrett_anderson_elizabeth.shtml>

"Women of the Hall: Elizabeth Blackwell." *National Women's Hall of Fame.* <http://www.greatwomen.org/women.php?action=viewone&id=20>

Glossary

abolitionist *(AB uh LIHSH uh nihst)* a person who favored the compulsory abolition of Negro slavery.

alternative medicine medicine that uses remedies and methods of treatment developed outside modern Western medicine.

anatomy *(uh NAT uh mee)* the science of the structure of animals and plants, based upon dissection, microscopic observation, and other analyses.

antiseptic *(AN tuh SEHP tihk)* preventing infection; unfavorable to the growth and activity of the microorganisms of disease, putrefaction, or fermentation.

apothecary *(uh POTH uh KEHR ee)* a person who prepares and sells drugs and medicines.

dispensary *(dihs PEHN suhr ee)* a place where medicines, medical care, and medical advice are given free or for a small charge.

dissection *(dih SEHK shuhn or dy SEHK shuhn)* the act of cutting apart an animal or plant, or any part of an animal or plant, in order to examine or study the structure.

forensic medicine the science that deals with the application of medical knowledge to certain questions of civil and criminal law.

gynecology *(GY nuh KOL uh jee)* the branch of medicine that deals with the functions and diseases specific to women, especially those of the reproductive system.

histology *(hihs TOL uh jee)* the branch of biology that deals with the structure, especially the microscopic structure, of the tissues of animals and plants.

inpatient *(IHN PAY shuhnt)* a patient who is lodged and fed in a hospital while undergoing treatment.

malaria *(muh LAIR ee uh)* a disease that causes chills, fever, and sweating. Malaria is transmitted by the bite of anopheles mosquitoes that have previously bitten infected persons.

midwifery *(MIHD WY fuhr ee, MIHD WYF ree, or MIHD wihf ree)* the art or practice of helping women in childbirth.

obstetrics *(ob STEHT rihks)* the branch of medicine and surgery concerned with treating women before, in, and after childbirth.

pathology *(puh THOL uh jee)* the study of the causes and nature of diseases, especially the structural and functional changes brought about by diseases.

pharmacist *(FAHR muh sihst)* a person licensed to fill prescriptions; druggist.

physiology *(FIHZ ee OL uh jee)* the science dealing with the normal functions of living things or their parts.

puerperal *(pyoo UR puhr uhl)* **fever** an infection of the mucous lining of the uterus occurring after childbirth.

suffragette *(SUHF ruh JEHT)* a woman supporter of the cause of suffrage for women.

temperance *(TEHM puhr uhns)* the principle and practice of not using alcoholic drinks.

toxicology *(TOK suh KOL uh jee)* the science that deals with poisons and their effects, antidotes, detection, etc.

transcendentalism *(TRAN sehn DEHN tuh lihz uhm)* the religious and philosophical doctrines of Ralph Waldo Emerson and others in New England in the middle 1800's, which emphasized the importance of individual inspiration and had an important influence on American thought and literature.

typhus *(TY fuhs)* an acute infectious disease characterized by high fever, extreme weakness, dark-red spots on the skin, and stupor or delirium. It is caused by a rickettsia carried by fleas, lice, ticks, or mites.

vivisection *(VIHV uh SEHK shuhn)* the act or practice of operating on living animals for scientific study or experimentation.

Index

Page numbers in *italic* type refer to pictures.

Garrett, Newson, 7-8, *8*, 10-12, 16, 23
Geneva Medical College, 53-58
germ theory of disease, 19-20, 67, 86-87

H
Hawes, William, 12
Heckford, Nathaniel, 15, 17
holistic medicine, 86-87
Human Element in Sex, The (Blackwell), 85
hydropathy, 64-65
hygiene, *57*, 75, 78, 82, 85

J
Jex-Blake, Sophia, 21-22, 84

K
Keiller, Alexander, 15
Kinney, Sara Thomson, 97

L
La Flesche, Joseph, Jr. (Iron Eye), 90-93, 98
La Flesche, Marguerite, 89, *92*, 94, 98, 101
La Flesche, Susette, 89, 93-94, *94*
La Maternitè, 60-62, *62*
Laws of Life with Special Reference to the Physical Education of Girls (Blackwell), 69
Lister, Sir Joseph, 20, *20*
Little, L. S., 15
London Hospital, 15
London School of Medicine for Women: Anderson at, 21-24, *22*, 25; Blackwell at, 84-86

M
Middlesex Hospital, 12-15
midwifery, 48, 60-61
Mill, John Stuart, *11*

N
National Health Society, 83
New Hospital for Women, 19, *19*, 23-24, 83
New York Infirmary for Indigent Women and Children, 73-75, 79-80
Nightingale, Florence, 66, *66*-67, 77-79
Norton, A. T., 23

O
Omaha people: alcoholism as problem among, 92, 99-101; Joseph La Flesche, Jr. as chief of, 91-93;

Picotte as advocate with government for, 102-104; Picotte as missionary to, 102; Picotte as reservation doctor for, 99-101, *100*; Picotte gives legal and financial help to, 100-101
ovariotomy, 86

P
Perkins, James H., 48
Picotte, Henry, 101-102, 105
Picotte, Susan La Flesche, 89-105; alcoholism fought by, 99-100; as advocate for Omaha with government, 102-104; as doctor at boarding school for Omaha Agency, 98-99; as first Native American woman doctor, 89; as missionary to Omaha people, 102; as reservation doctor, 99-101, *100*; at Hampton Normal and Agricultural Institute, 95-96; at Woman's Medical College of Pennsylvania, 96-98; children of, 102, *104*; death of, 105; decides to become a doctor, 94-96; education of, 93-96; English learned by, 93; health problems of, 101-102, 104-105; hospital for Omaha people built by, 105; internship at Woman's Hospital, Philadelphia, 98; legal and financial help given to Omaha by, 100-101; marriage to Henry Picotte, 101; medical practice in Nebraska, 101-102; on progress for Indians, 96; parents of, 90-91; photograph of 1880, *92*; sisters and brothers of, 89
Pioneer Work in Opening the Medical Profession to Women (Blackwell), 85
preventive medicine, 82-83
prostitution, 67
Punch (magazine), 88

R
record-keeping, 75

S
St. Mary's Dispensary for Women and Children, 16
sanitary visitor, 82
sanitation, 20, 57, 82-83
Scharlieb, Mary, 23
Scientific Method in Biology (Blackwell), 85
Selection and Training of Nurses, The (Blackwell), 80

sex education, 67-69
sexually transmitted diseases, 56
slavery, Blackwell's opposition to, 30, 34-36, 40-41, 43-44, 51
Smith, Barbara Leigh (Bodichon), 10, 66, 76, 82-83, 87
Society of Apothecaries, 14-16
Stowe, Harriet Beecher, 39, 45, 48, 74
suffrage for women, *11*, 24

T
Transcendentalism, 40-41

V
vivisection, 24, 85-86

W
Waldron, Martha M., 95, 97
Warrington, Joseph, 52, 54
Webster, James, 55, 58
Woman's Central Association of Relief, 80, *81*
Woman's Hospital (Philadelphia), 98
Woman's Medical College of Pennsylvania, 96-98
women: education for, 12, 31, 46-47; idealization of, 46-47; lack of opportunities for educated, 78; occupations open to, 47; recognition not given their accomplishments, 76; suffrage, *11*, 24; Victorian view of, 31
women doctors: Anderson as first female doctor in Great Britain, 7; Blackwell as first woman to earn M.D. degree, 58; British Medical Association excluding women, 21; British Medical Council bars women, 77; French doctors as dismissive of, 60; landlords refuse to rent offices to, 68; medical colleges for women opening, 67, 75; men seeing as professional rivals, 53; need for, 10; obstacles to becoming, 11; Picotte as first Native American, 89; seen as inappropriate, 13; women seen as too weak for, 48
Women's Medical College of the New York Infirmary, 81-82, *86*
Wrong and Right Methods of Dealing with Social Evil (Blackwell), 85

Z
Zakrzewska, Marie, 71-75, 79